WOMEN
OF THE
WAR YEARS

WOMEN IN BRITAIN
1939 TO 1945

WOMEN

OF THE

WAR YEARS

WOMEN IN BRITAIN
1939 TO 1945

JANICE ANDERSON

Futura

A Futura Book

First published by Futura in 2009

Copyright © Omnipress 2009

ISBN: 978-0-7088-0059-1

Produced by Omnipress Ltd, United Kingdom

Printed in Singapore

Futura
An imprint of
Little, Brown Book Group
100 Victoria Embankment
London EC4Y 0DY

An Hachette UK Company

Photo credits: Getty Images

CONTENTS

AT WAR AGAIN

When the United Kingdom's prime minister, Neville Chamberlain announced on the wireless on 3 September 1939 that the country was at war with Germany, it was for the second time in the twentieth century – and with the same enemy. The difference this time, as Mother and Home *magazine put it in their November 1939 issue, was that 'the last was a soldier's war. This one is Everybody's'.*

It had been clear for much of the 1930s that Britain was likely to be caught up in a war again with the increasingly aggressive Germany of Adolf Hitler and the National Socialists. The British government and its officials all agreed that such a war, if it were to be fought to a victorious end, would have to involve everyone, including women. Nazi Germany's ideal woman, tied to home, kitchen and children, did not play well in government war-planning offices in Britain.

This is not to say that Britain's male-dominated governing class was unsympathetic towards the German 'ideal woman', it was

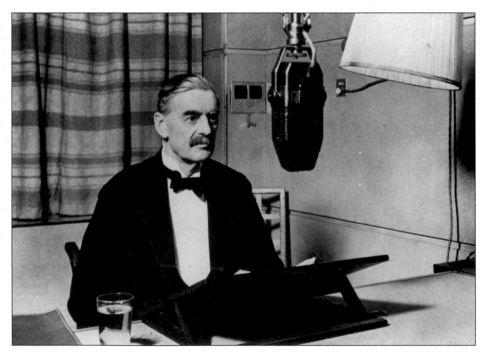

▲ *TELLING THE COUNTRY*
British Prime Minister Neville Chamberlain (1869–1940) in a BBC studio announcing the declaration of war.

▲ *SHOPPERS QUEUE FOR THEIR FISH IN ELTHAM*
This particular shopkeeper has posted a notice that only local people will be served and identity
cards inspected before the purchase can be made.

just that they knew it would not work in wartime. It was every British woman's patriotic duty to serve the country in any way she could in wartime, to respond to a national emergency. In no way did this imply that, once peace had returned, women should not also return to their pre-war lives.

This attitude was so ingrained that, well into the war, it allowed Prime Minister Winston Churchill to say that women who were asking for the same pay as their male colleagues in the teaching profession were being 'impertinent'. As late as 1944, an official government publication dealing with mobilisation in Britain and called, ironically enough, *Man Power*, said that 'the whole business of mobilising and employing women – wives, sweethearts and daughters – is new and tricky. It creates special and dangerous problems…over and above those encountered in the conscription and mobilisation of men.'

'Sweetheart' was an attractively romantic way to refer to young women, used most famously as the label for perhaps the best-known and most admired woman in wartime Britain, warm-voiced singer Vera Lynn, the 'Forces' Sweetheart'. But it was also a very old-fashioned word, harking back to Victorian and Edwardian days. It did not suggest the modern woman that 1930s feminists were trying to promote.

This inability to see women as simply potential workers – nobody thought there was anything 'tricky' about the fact that male workers were also 'husbands, lovers and sons' – would take more than six years of war to eradicate from male-dominated official thinking. It was, however, well buried during the war: the only country that was more effective than the United Kingdom in mobilising women to help 'win the Peace' was the Soviet Union. And the USSR went a step further than even the British were prepared to go, sending their women to fight in their armed forces.

Thousands of British women joined the auxiliary army, navy and air force services or their nursing and medical units, during the war, and did essential, invaluable work at home and abroad. Thousands more worked in Civil Defence, courting danger and risking death day and night in London, and also in the country's industrial cities and dockyards – the destruction of which was the Germany Luftwaffe's main aim. The number of women in the Women's Land Army and the Timber Corps had reached nearly 85,000 by mid-1943. Then there were the thousands of women who worked in industry and who were, especially if they worked in munitions factories, just as likely to be the targets of German bombers as were their sisters in Civil Defence.

Perhaps Britain's greatest asset in its fight against Hitler's Germany was its vast army of housewives. While remaining true to the 'women as homemakers' ideal, housewives took up the enormous challenges wartime threw at them without flinching. Most of them suddenly found themselves on their own, in sole charge of their households which might well include, as well as their own children, evacuees, billeted workers, and relatives bombed out of their homes. They quickly dealt with all the business of protecting their homes from damage, especially by incendiary bombs.

They queued for hours in all weathers outside shops, clutching the ration books for everyone in their household, and then, probably, queuing for hours more for a bus to get their shopping home. As the war went on,

▲ *FORCES'-- SWEETHEART*
The popular British singer Vera Lynn became the Forces' sweetheart.

▲ *PIG FOOD COLLECTOR*
A worker from the Women's Voluntary Service supervises a woman as she empties household waste into a separate rubbish bin for pig feed, a novel scheme in the London borough of Westminster.

they learnt how to make nourishing meals with less and less – and thought nothing of serving them on top of the Morrison shelter which took up so much room that the dining table had had to make way for it. They became adept at growing their own vegetables, even on the roof of the Anderson shelter in the garden, and at keeping hens and pigs, carefully saving all their food waste either for their own pig or for the pig-swill bins that were put out on the pavements. They made do and mended so that they and their children were neatly and warmly, if not always fashionably, dressed.

As well as all this, most housewives found time to do their bit for the war effort outside the home, perhaps by joining the WVS, or working in Red Cross shops or the new Citizen Advice Bureau information centres. They drove ambulances, worked in canteens, British Restaurants and emergency feeding centres. They joined savings groups and became part-time air-raid wardens. There was very little that the ordinary housewife was not able to do if she put her mind to it.

The war over, most women left the services, the munitions factories, the hospitals and all their other wartime jobs to become housewives again: by 1951 the numbers of women in full-time employment had returned to 1939 levels, but now Britain was a welfare state, with good education and health systems available to all. There was also increasing prosperity for all, a prosperity that, to be enjoyed, had to be paid for. Women had learned how to hold down jobs while running a home during the war and they were prepared to do so again, to ensure that they and their families could enjoy the new prosperity that the new Elizabethan Age, and its female head of state, Elizabeth II, promised them.

1939

JANUARY
- Physicists Lise Meitner and Otto R. Frisch describe the process called 'nuclear fission'.

FEBRUARY
- The German battleship *Bismarck* is launched.

MARCH
- Germany invades the remainder of Czechoslovakia.
- Italy invades Albania.

MARCH
- Spanish Civil War ends as Madrid falls to Francisco Franco.

MARCH
- Britain and France join forces.

AUGUST
- Germany and Russia sign a mutual non-aggression pact.

SEPTEMBER
- Germany invades Poland.
- British warship *Athenia* is sunk by Germany U-boats off the coast of Ireland.
- Britain and France officially declare war on Germany.
- American aviator Charles A. Lindbergh makes his first anti-war radio speech.
- Poland is partitioned between Germany and Russia.

OCTOBER
- Hitler starts his euthanasia on the sick and disabled in Germany.

NOVEMBER
- A Neutrality Act is signed allowing America to send arms and aid to Britain and France.
- An assassination attempt on Hitler in Munich fails.
- Russian troops invade Finland.
- Talks on building an atomic bomb for Germany.

DECEMBER
- The National Women's Party meets in Washington and urges the Congress to act on an Equal Rights Amendment.

AN ARMY OF WOMEN VOLUNTEERS

In May 1941, three government departments combined to produce a leaflet called 'Beating the Invader' which was issued to everyone in Britain. It began with a message from the Prime Minister. 'If invasion comes, everyone – young or old, men and women – will be eager to play their part worthily,' wrote Winston Churchill, going on to say that there would be two duties for everyone: STAND FIRM and CARRY ON. In truth, many of Britain's women had been playing their part, carrying on with their lives but also making some firm decisions about their behaviour in wartime, since the Munich Crisis of 1938, when war had suddenly seemed so close.

▲ *BLACKOUT MATERIAL*
People bought blackout material and sticky tape to prepare their windows for war.

When war did finally come in 1939, thousands of women up and down the land already had well-stocked larders, had bought the blackout materials and sticky tape necessary to prepare their windows for war, knew how to wear the gas masks that had already been issued to adults and children at the time of the Munich crisis (babies got theirs, in the form of a bag into which the baby had to be put, in September 1939), and had made practical plans for a bomb shelter, even if it could only be a very sturdy table in the kitchen. No-one, having seen the effects of aerial bombing on the cities of Spain during the Civil War of 1936, was in any doubt that if war came to Britain, then everyone, civilian or serviceman, was in danger of attack from bombs and gas.

However, there was also a strong feeling that simply guarding the home would not be enough. Again and again, the same theme turns up in the diaries and journals, letters to friends and articles in newspapers and magazines written before and during the war: most British women believed it was their patriotic duty to make a contribution to the war effort, while still doing their best to guard their children and families from harm.

The most serious 'volunteering' decision faced by many women some months before the war started, was whether or not, should war come, to allow their older children, as well as themselves if they had babies, to be evacuated from the parts of the country – the capital, large urban and industrial areas and dockyards – the government had designated as Evacuation Areas. Mothers and babies and school-age children, with their school classes and teachers, would be evacuated to so-called Reception Areas, mostly on the coasts well away from Europe

1940

JANUARY
- Japan bombs the Chinese city of Ningbo with fleas carrying the bubonic plague.
- 250 gypsies are killed in the Buchenweld concentration camp.
- Germany creates a Jewish ghetto in Lodz, Poland.
- Russia bombs cities in Finland.

FEBRUARY
- Russia commences bombing of Sweden.
- The German tanker *Altmark*, with 299 British prisoners, was boarded in neutral Norwegian waters by sailors from the British destroyer HMS *Cossack* and the prisoners set free.

MARCH
- Hitler and Mussolini form an alliance with Italy against Britain and France.

APRIL
- Operation Weseruebung – Germany invades Denmark and Norway.
- Russia massacres 15,000 Polish officers in the woods at Katyn.

MAY
- Germany invades Belgium and Holland.
- British Prime Minister Neville Chamberlain resigns and is replaced by Winston Churchill.
- Start of the Germany *Blitzkrieg* (lightning war).
- Germany invades France.
- Holland surrenders.
- Britain bombs Bremen and Hamburg, while the German army reaches the English Channel.
- Britain evacuates 300,000 troops from Dunkerque.
- Belgium surrenders.

JUNE
- Italy declares war on Britain and France.

1940 continued . . .

JUNE
• German troops enter Paris.
• Norway surrenders.
• German concentration camp is set up at Auschwitz in Poland.
• Russia invades Estonia, Latvia and Lithuania.
• France surrenders to Germany and Philippe Petain leads a new government.

JULY
• Germany bombs Britain.

AUGUST
• Germany commences a bombing campaign which kills hundreds of people every day.
• Exiled Russian revolutionary Leon Trotsky is fatally wounded in Mexico City by an assassin's ice-ax and dies the next day.

SEPTEMBER
• Italy invades Egypt.
• Germany, Italy and Japan sign the 'Axis' treaty.

▲ *CANADA BOUND*
Children and young women being evacuated to Canada circa 1941.

and the North Sea or in rural areas. Because the evacuation scheme was voluntary, the Government put a large propaganda programme into effect, plastering the Evacuation Areas with posters aimed directly at mothers. 'MOTHERS Send Them Out of London, Give them a chance of greater safety and health' the words of a poster used in London, was typical of the approach used on such posters and in leaflets.

Giving a home to children evacuated from the danger zones of the big cities and ports was the first opportunity to help the war effort given to many women. The WVS set up an Evacuation Committee within weeks

of its founding in 1938 and by 1939 had its local groups well organised to deal with the business of receiving evacuees. WVS local evacuation committees usually included members of other organisations, such as the Girl Guides and the Women's Institutes. For the first evacuation wave, local committees had little trouble in finding enough houses to take in evacuees. Most women were ready to help. Even the writer Virginia Woolf and her husband Leonard found room in their home at Rodmell, Sussex for evacuees. She noted in her diary for 6 September that 'we have carried coals etc into the cottage for the eight Battersea women and children. The expectant mothers are all quarrelling.'

▲ *EVACUEES LEAVING LONDON*
Labelled evacuees waiting for their train out of London. About eight million people, including children and their mothers, were evacuated from cities and industrial areas during World War II.

THE THREE EVACUATIONS

There were three waves of evacuations from vulnerable areas during the war. The first began on 1 September 1939. During the three days of this evacuation some 1.5 million people, the majority of them children, were evacuated to safer parts of the country and out of the country altogether, many to Canada. Because the declaration of war was followed by nearly seven months of the Phoney War, when nothing much happened at home, more than 60 per cent of children were brought home by their parents. The Blitz led to a second wave of evacuation, much more smoothly organised than the first, between May and December 1940. The third wave was caused by the V1 flying bomb ('doodlebug') and the V2 rocket attacks, which began in June 1944 and did not end until March 1945. About eight million people, including children, their mothers, disabled people and some overseas refugees, were evacuated from cities and industrial areas during World War II.

The sudden arrival into their homes of groups of children, especially if those children came from the slums and tenements of deprived inner city areas, was an extraordinarily disturbing business for many householders – and for the children who came into their homes. Many children from really deprived areas did not know how to hold a knife and fork and were unfamiliar with the simple but healthy foods put in front of them. There were numerous reports of children, never having seen a toilet, urinating on carpets.

Mrs Nella Last's comments in the diary she kept for Mass-Observation were typical of many heard again and again throughout Britain. 'The country and village people have

▼ *FEMALE HANDS TO THE DECK*
Members of the WVS at Winchmore Hill working at St Paul's Institute making camouflage nets which were urgently required for war purposes.

1940 continued . . .

SEPTEMBER
• Germany invades Romania.
• The USS *Greer* becomes the first United States ship fired upon by a German submarine in the war.

OCTOBER
• Conscription begins in the US.
• Germany invades Romania.
• Italy invades Greece.

NOVEMBER
• Hungary, Romania and Slovakia enter the war on the side of Germany.
• Franklin D. Roosevelt is re-elected as president of the United States.
• Germany builds a walled ghetto for the 500,000 Jews of Warsaw, Poland.

DECEMBER
• Britain commence Operation Compass against the Italians In North Africa. Over 20,000 Italians are taken prisoner.

had the shock of their lives with the sample of children and mothers who have been billeted on them from Manchester and Salford,' she wrote. 'One little boy of eight, after assuring the women that the dirt "would not come off" his legs and neck, was forcibly bathed with hot water and carbolic.… There is a run on Keating's [flea powder] and disinfectant and soap, while children who arrived with a crop of curls look like shorn lambs – but have stopped scratching!'

Although the evacuation scheme turned out to be a traumatic experience in many cases, for both the evacuated children and their mothers and for the people who gave them homes, for others evacuation turned out to be a happy experience for both parties. In the long run, the experience of evacuation during World War II and its revelation of the depths of poverty existing in many parts of Britain led to a complete reorganisation of social services, starting, at the height of the war, with the Beveridge Report in 1942-3 and the establishment of the post-war Welfare State. There were two more waves of evacuation during the war, notably in 1944 when the V1 and V2 weapons began raining down on England, while volunteering to look after children continued to be important 'war effort' work for many women. As one war-time poster had it, 'If you can't go to the factory help the neighbour who can. Caring for war workers' children is a national service.'

◀ *ROCKET INJURIES*
When a V-2 rocket fell on Smithfield Market in Farringdon Road, London on 8 March 1945, it killed 380 people and many more were injured. This picture was not published until fourteen years later as it was feared it would have a detrimental effect on morale.

1941

JANUARY
• Britain and Australia invade Libya.
FEBRUARY
• Britain invades Somalia.
• Rommel is appointed as commander of the German army in Africa.
• 100,000 Jews are deported from Vienna.
• First gold record presented to Glenn Miller for *Chattanooga Choo Choo*.
MARCH
• Bulgaria joins the war in support of Germany.
APRIL
• Iraq joins the war on the side of Germany.
• Germany invades Yugoslavia and Greece.
• Croatia declares its independence and Yugoslavia enters the war in support of Germany.
• Russia and Japan sign a non-aggression pact.
• German troops enter Athens.
MAY
• Italy surrenders in Africa.
• Britain enters Baghdad.
• Britain invades Syria and Lebanon to prevent them being taken over by Germany.
• Emperor Haile Selassie returns to Addis Ababa and since then the date has been celebrated as Liberation Day.
JUNE
• Germany breaks the non-aggression pact with Russia and commences Operation Barbarossa.
• Italy and Romania declare war on Germany.
• Finland and Hungary declare war on Russia.
JULY
• Japan invades Indochina.
• Italy attacks Valetta harbour in Malta.
• Mass murder of Polish scientists and writers by Nazies.

LATEST PRICES · ITS CLEAR Nicholson's Gin ITS GOOD · **Evening Standard** · LATE NIGHT FINAL · La Coquille · No. 35,880 LONDON, FRIDAY, SEPTEMBER 1, 1939 ONE PENNY

HELPING TO FEED COVENTRY

The first Queen's Messengers Convoy to go into action went to Coventry from Lewisham, in south London, in November 1940. The convoy consisted of four motor cyclists, eight lorries and twenty-seven WVS women, many of whom had had to leave a scribbled note on the kitchen table for their families, as they had packed up for the journey in such haste. By 7 a.m. on the morning after they had left London, they were already in action, distributing hot drinks and sandwiches to the rescue workers and ignoring the delayed action bombs going off all over the ravaged city. In the two days they were in Coventry this first Queen's Messengers Convoy prepared and served fourteen thousand meals to the people of Coventry, while their cups of tea helped wash the blood and dust out of the mouths of the men who were digging the trapped people – and the bodies – out of the rubble.

The women's volunteer organisation that contributed most to the war effort at home was the Women's Voluntary Service (WVS). Well before September 1939, women in Britain had been joining volunteer organisations in their thousands, with many choosing to do first aid and nurse aiding work with the Red Cross or the St John Ambulance Association, but it was the WVS that attracted the most women volunteers, throughout the war and for some time afterwards. The WVS was formed in 1938, the brainchild of Stella Isaacs, Dowager Marchioness of Reading, primarily to assist civil defence organisations and to provide welfare in the event of war.

As the blue, white and black card many WVS members displayed in the front windows of their homes said, the WVS was a 'housewives service' of Britain's wartime Civil Defence. Where the volunteers of such Civil Defence organisations as ARP and the AFS did much of their work while the air raids and bombings were still going on, the WVS was in the forefront of dealing with the aftermath of air raids and the other results of war. Almost all the hundreds of thousands of women – their numbers were never officially counted – who wore the

▶ *MOBILE CANTEEN*
Boys drinking tea and eating sandwiches in front of a Food Flying Squad mobile canteen at Coventry, part of the Queen's Messenger Food Convoy. Supported by US aid, the service, staffed by the WVS, provided food for people made homeless by German bombing raids.

grey-green uniform suits, coats, berets and felt hats of the WVS during the second world war were paid nothing more than out-of-pocket expenses for their heroic services.

Even before war was declared, the WVS was organising greeters and helpers for the thousands of children evacuated from the perceived danger zones from the first day of September. Soon, they were also helping to provide clothing for the evacuees. Then in 1940, when thousands of troops were suddenly arriving from the horrors of Dunkirk at ports in Kent and along the south coast, the women of the WVS found themselves washing the feet and darning the socks of thousands of exhausted soldiers, while also serving thousands of meals and cups of tea.

A welcome sight in many bomb-damaged cities during the Blitz was a Queen's Messengers Convoy. There were eighteen of these Queen's Messengers Convoys, the first one paid for by Queen Elizabeth – hence the convoys' name – and most of the rest of them paid for by overseas generosity, especially American. Each convoy consisted of up to twelve vehicles, equipped to rush hot meals, drinks and fresh water to bombed areas. They were manned by members of the WVS and did particularly valuable work in

1941 continued . . .

AUGUST
• Roosevelt and Churchill begin secret meetings off the coast of Newfoundland, resulting in the Atlantic Charter.
• Britain and Russia invade Iran.

SEPTEMBER
• Roosevelt orders that all German or Italian ships sighted in US waters must be destroyed.
• Germany invades the Ukraine. Between 50,000 and 96,000 Ukranians are machine gunned to death in the Babi Yar ravine.

OCTOBER
• A US destroyer, the *Kearny*, torpedoed off the coast of Iceland by a German U-boat.
• General Hideki Tojo is appointed prime minister of Japan.
• Another destroyer, the *Reuben James*, is sunk by a German U-boat, killing 100 people.

▶ *REFUGEE CLOTHING*
Two WVS volunteers wheel bales of clothing away from the baling department of the Women's Voluntary Service Clothing Depot, to be sent to refugees in various countries.

Coventry, Liverpool and Plymouth in the later months of the Blitz.

The WVS's main task during the Blitz was to provide strong back-up support for the Civil Defence services. Their locally-maintained censuses were invaluable for ARP people assessing the population of bombed streets and houses and they became very practised at organising convoys out of bombed areas. The WVS canteen van, many of which were donated by other countries, including the Dominions, the West Indies and Kenya, became a familiar sight in the middle of clearing-up operations after a bombing raid. The WVS canteens provided refreshments for both the casualties of bombing raids and the Civil Defence workers helping with the clearing-up operations. Members of the WVS also became adept at showing people how to build makeshift brick ovens in the street using the rubble from bombed-out buildings.

Perhaps not quite as familiar a sight as the canteen van, but just as welcome when it did turn up, was the mobile laundry service units that the WVS manned in bomb-damaged housing areas. In Portsmouth, where sixty-five thousand out of the city's total housing stock of seventy thousand were either destroyed or damaged by enemy action, mobile laundries were essential. Rescued clothes and bedlinen would be

FROM MEN'S SUITING INTO BLANKETS

'I went to the WVS Centre today [5 September 1939] and was amazed at the huge crowd. We have moved into a big room in the middle of town now, but big as it was, every table was crowded uncomfortably with eager workers. Afterwards… dozens of books of tailor's patterns to be machined together [for blankets] were taken. [A blanket averages] about seventy-seven yards of machining to join each piece with a double row of stitching and a double-stitched hem. I'm on my third big one and have made about a dozen cot quilts. As my husband says, it would have been quicker to walk the distance than machine it. I'm lucky, for my machine is electric and so does not tire me.' – from the diary that Mrs Nella Last, a Barrow-in-Furness housewife, kept for Mass-Observation throughout the war. Mrs Last had decided within a week of the war's start that she would dedicate every part of her time when not looking after her husband to the WVS. Her diary was published as *Nella Last's War* (Profile Books, 2006).

washed in the units and hung out to dry on lines, hopefully under cover but quite often strung across streets and between bombed-out houses. Many of these units were provided by the manufacturer of the popular washing powder, Rinso, doing its bit to keep the nation's washing clean even if many of the nation's domestic washing machines were being destroyed by the enemy.

At the height of the Blitz in London, local authority rest centres, housed in church halls, schools, office buildings and many other places and manned largely by WVS women, were sheltering around twenty-five thousand people who had been bombed out of their houses. The WVS's national structure geared itself to organising the training of its volunteers in many essentials, from first aid and ambulance work, to cooking for large numbers and sorting and distributing clothes by the ton. By 1941, the WVS's work had moved in directions unimagined in 1938. After Lord Beaverbrook's appeal for household aluminium to help the aircraft industry, it was the WVS which set up pots-and-pans collecting depots in towns and cities. The response of WVS groups in Sussex to the 'Beating the Invader' leaflet was to organise a messenger service of women cyclists who would be able to maintain communications if the invader blocked roads and cut telegraph lines.

For the many thousands of men, women and children who survived a bombing raid with nothing but the clothes they stood up in, the WVS's nationwide network of shops and depots was a godsend. During the war, the WVS centre was the main source of replacement clothing and blankets for people whose homes had been severely damaged or destroyed. WVS clothing centres also provided warm sweaters, scarves, gloves and balaclavas, many of them knitted by WVS members, for the seamen of the Royal Navy and the merchant navy fighting the war at sea in the North Atlantic. Although a lot of the clothing donated to the WVS came from British people, much of it came from America and the Dominions of the Empire, especially Australia, Canada, New Zealand and South Africa. In the second half of 1940, when the Blitz was at its height, the WVS distributed clothing worth around £1.5 million.

By the time the Blitz came to an end in London in May 1941, 241 WVS members had been killed in the bombing, and many more injured. Twenty-five WVS offices and centres had been destroyed, and, of course, there were WVS casualties in many other cities. By this time, over one million women had enrolled in the WVS. The Housewives Service grew considerably during the Blitz, and by the time it was renamed the Housewives Section in 1942, it accounted for 20 per cent of the membership of the whole WVS.

The WVS continued throughout the war and after to be a major force in local voluntary services. In April 1945, as the Home Secretary and his Scottish counterpart announced in the House of Commons, the WVS would be fitted into the general pattern of Social Services throughout the country, with its work supported from central funds.

▶ *HANGING UP THE WASHING*
Members of the WVS working in the Laundry can be seen here hanging out army shirts to dry, from Aldershot Barracks, Surrey. The laundry workers washed over 1500 army shirts a week.

DOING MEN'S WORK
IN WAR TIME

During World War II, workers in the armaments factories and dockyards of Britain and her allies from the Empire – Australia, Canada, New Zealand and South Africa – provided the Allied cause with 700 warships and thousands of merchant ships, 135,000 aircraft and more than 160,000 tanks and other armoured vehicles. Nearly seven million of the twenty million or so workers involved were women.

The call-up of men of suitable age not in reserved occupations meant that it was inevitable, as it had been in World War I, that women would have to be employed to work in the men's places. About five million women in Britain had paid jobs in September 1939. Many of them would have stayed at home but for the fact that the depression of the 1930s put many men and breadwinners out of work. When the war started in 1930, the government made cutbacks in non-essential industries, closing many factories or else making them re-tool to produce essential war-time goods. While many women found themselves making munitions, rather than furniture or fabrics, for instance, nearly 175,000 women found themselves without a job of any kind.

Thus, many women, especially among those who had left school at fourteen to work in factories, were in a position to volunteer for work that would really help the war effort: if your work as a fifteen-year-old involved cutting out the satin linings that went into cutlery boxes, then work in a factory producing things important to the war effort sounded interesting, even attractive – and, of course, it could be work that might involve more money than you had earned in your old job.

At the start of the war, women's readiness to take on jobs previously done by men was not matched by the Government's eagerness to employ them, well aware as it was of the trade unions' antipathy towards allowing women to take over men's jobs. Among men workers, few of whom felt the jingoistic patriotism that had swept young men into the recruiting offices in August 1914, there was a similar reluctance to see women on the machines or the assembly lines next to them. Then there was the wide-spread belief

▶ *WOMAN'S WORK*
This woman is grinding a 6-pounder tank gun barrel at a British factory where over 650 women were employed in order to release the men for the services during wartime.

A MORALE-BOOSTER FROM THE RAF

Attempts to sap the morale of Britain's munitions workers played a major part in the broadcasts from Germany made by Lord Haw Haw (the notorious traitor William Joyce who fled to Germany in 1939), but his taunts were seldom left unanswered. Phyllis Pearson, an artist and map-maker, was given a pass allowing her to draw the workers – 'absolutely superb women [whose] morale was high even though they were working under unbelievable pressure' – in a munitions factory in Blackburn. She recalled nearly fifty years later, for the broadcaster and journalist Mavis Nicholson, how one particular broadcast by Lord Haw Haw was swiftly countered. Lord Haw Haw had said, after the Battle of El Alamein, that the shells from British munitions factories could not pierce the armour of German tanks being chased across the Western Desert. Just two days after Lord Haw Haw's broadcast, photographs taken by the RAF in North Africa clearly showing German tanks wrecked by British shells were put up in the factory.

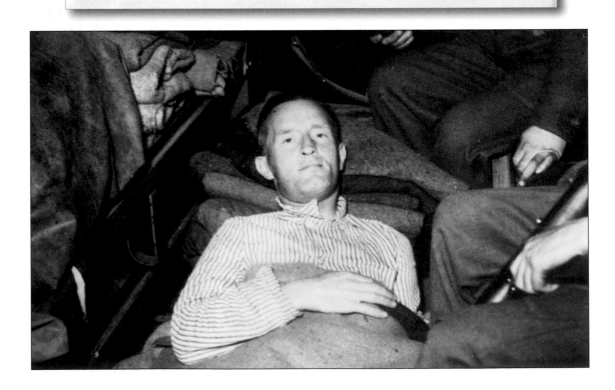

that women, being physically inferior, would not be able to do men's work well or efficiently. An extension of this argument was the feeling that women would never deserve to be paid the same as men. Even more serious was the fear that putting women to work would be a real danger to home and family life. When would houses be cleaned, food bought, and meals provided for children and husbands returning from their reserved occupation work?

As the war went on and the great contribution that women were making to the civilian war effort was recognised, much of the sting went out of such arguments. As the popular song of 1942 put it: 'it's the girl that makes the thing that holds the oil that oils the ring, that works the thingumebob that's going to win the war'.

With men disappearing into the armed forces in increasing numbers, the need for women to replace them became increasingly urgent, especially in armaments and munitions factories. At the beginning of the war, women already with jobs were expected to simply carry on with them. They could volunteer for more specifically war-related jobs if they wished. By January 1941, with the war no longer phoney, 'voluntaryism' was no longer enough, and the Ministry of Labour issued a Registration for Employment Order that directed all men and women between the ages of eighteen and sixty-five

◀ *LORD HAW HAW*
Born in America of Irish parents, British traitor and broadcaster William Joyce (Lord Haw Haw) can be seen here surrounded by armed guards as he arrives on a stretcher at a hospital near Luneberg. He was executed for his treasonable support of the Nazi cause.

▲ *MUNITIONS WORK*
Women were called up for war work from March 1941 and, although there were many different types of jobs, many went to work in munitions factories. Above is a woman at work in a London munitions factory producing Bren guns and other small arms

1941

NOVEMBER
- Germany attacks Moscow.
- British aircraft carrier *Ark Royal* is sunk off Gibraltar by German U-boat.

DECEMBER
- Britain declares war on Finland.
- The USA declares an oil embargo against Japan.
- The Japanese attack Pearl Harbor. The attack cripples the US Pacific fleet and kills more than 2,300 US soldiers, sailors and civilians. The attack preceded Japan's formal declaration of war.
- Japan invades Thailand and Malaysia.
- Roosevelt signs the declaration of war.
- Britain and the USA declare war on Japan.
- Japan invades the Philippines.
- Egypt, Mexico, Panama and Cuba declare war on Japan.
- Germany and Italy declare war on the USA.
- Bulgaria, Hungary, Croatia, Slovakia and Romania declare war on the USA.
- Japan captures Hong Kong on Christmas Day.

When you see a rattlesnake poised to strike you, do not wait until he has struck before you crush him.

FRANKLIN D. ROOSEVELT (1882–1945). Thirty-second President of the USA.

to register for war work, with the proviso that at this time the order applied only to women aged twenty and twenty-one.

For the first time, British women, albeit at first in a narrow age-band, could be directed to jobs, for which they began registering at employment agencies from the spring of 1941. By August 1941, eighty-seven thousand women, out of what was thought to be a potential women's workforce of two million, had been given jobs in the auxiliary services and in munitions. But this was still not enough to fill the nation's huge need for workers. After months of deliberation, the government decided to bring in conscription for women. When the National Service (No. 2) Act became law in December 1941, it not only made war work compulsory for women, it made Britain the first nation in modern times to conscript women. At this stage, the Act applied only to women aged twenty to thirty; in the following year, nineteen-year-olds were also called up. Women could be conscripted into the auxiliary services, into industry or into farm work (although with the last two, employment exchanges continued to use the term 'direct' rather than 'conscript').

By 1943, nearly ninety per cent of single women aged between eighteen and forty and about eighty per cent of married women were doing war work of some kind, about seven million of them in full-time civilian jobs. In May 1943, part-time work, which could mean up to thirty hours a week, became compulsory for all women aged from eighteen to forty-five, unless they still had children under fourteen at home. If a woman's children were all fourteen or over, then she was considered able to take on work outside the home.

▲ *WARTIME HARVEST*
A group of land girls bringing in sheaves of wheat from a field reclaimed for the war effort from four hundred acres of unused land on the Sussex Downs. The field is thought to have been the largest of its kind in Britain.

▲ NERVE CENTRE
Women from the Auxiliary Fire Service at work in the London Fire Regional Control Room, where the mobilising of fire appliances was carried out by means of maps.

Quite a lot of part-time work was actually undertaken at home. Groups of women might gather round the table in one of their houses to do essential work, such as sorting into sizes rivets, screws and other small items used in munitions and aircraft factories, which could be done outside the factories. It allowed women to make a valuable contribution to the war effort while also maintaining a proper family home.

There was an irony about the fourteen-year-old cut-off point for dependent children: if the war had not happened in September 1939 all fourteen-year-olds would have had to return to school for the start of the new year as that had been decided on as the date for raising the school leaving age to fifteen. As it was, many fourteen-year-old former schoolgirls found themselves doing a wide range of responsible jobs, from delivering telegrams and helping in first aid posts to fire-fighting and other forms of civil defence. The youngest person to be awarded a George Medal during World War II was fourteen-year-old Charity Bick, who won the medal for her outstanding bravery during a heavy air raid on Birmingham in February 1941. Charity should not

▼ *FIRE FIGHTERS*
It wasn't just in Britain that women were called into the fire service. This picture shows women directing a hose after the Japanese attack on the US naval base at Pearl Harbor.

1942

JANUARY
- Japanese troops capture Manila.
- Japan invades Indonesia.
- Britain counter-attacks in North Africa.
- Churchill and Roosevelt hold a conference at Casablanca.
- Japan invades Burma.
- German U-boats attack the USA.
- Roosevelt orders that all immigrants register with the government. It is the start of a plan to move Japanese-Americans to internment camps.
- USA sends the first troops to Britain.

FEBRUARY
- Japanese troops capture Singapore.
- Germany makes plans for the 'final solution' to exterminate all Jews.
- Roosevelt signs an order authorising the transfer of over 100,000 Japanese-Americans to concentration camps.
- The Soviet Union commences a project for an atomic bomb under the guidance of Igor Vasilievich Kurchatov.
- The gas chamber is put into action at Auschwitz.

MARCH
- General MacArthur appointed Supreme Commander of Allied Forces in the Southwest Pacific Area.
- Lord Mountbatten appointed Chief of Combined Operations.

APRIL
- The Philippines fall to Japanese troops.
- USA bombs Tokyo, Yokohama, Osaka-Kobe and Nagoya
- As a punishment to the villages who helped USA troops, operation Sei-Go kills 250,000 Chinese civilians.
- Coastal blackouts go into effect in response to German U-boat activity along the US Atlantic coast.

have been on duty at all; she told the ARP recruiting people that she was sixteen, in order to get a job as an ARP Services Despatch Rider.

In the early months of the war women beginning work in engineering, munitions and armaments factories found that, in many cases, the men they would eventually replace were still on the job, resentful at having to go to war anyway, and even more resentful of the women waiting to take their jobs. Again and again, women reported how difficult their first weeks and months were, trying to understand work and machines that were never fully explained to them in factories that were cold, unfriendly and uncomfortable places, and, more often than not, with insufficient lavatories and wash places for a suddenly greatly increased female work force.

Working away from home became a major issue for women during the war, and whether a women was 'mobile' or 'immobile' became an important employment exchange distinction. Their home commitments meant that many women had to stay within daily travelling distance of their work, while others, mostly young and with no family commitments, could find themselves sent almost anywhere in the country that had been designated a Demand Region for workers. (Britain was divided into eleven regions, designated either 'Supply' or 'Demand', by the Ministry of Labour.) If the woman was directed to a factory far from home, she could very likely find herself living in a hostel, a school or hall, commandeered as living accommodation for workers 'for the duration'.

Eventually, many women factory workers found themselves working up to sixty or

LATEST PRICES — LATE NIGHT FINAL
ITS CLEAR Nicholson's Gin ITS GOOD
Evening Standard
La Coquille
No. 35,800   LONDON, FRIDAY, SEPTEMBER 1, 1939   ONE PENNY

A MAN'S WAGE FOR A MAN'S JOB

Some women doing men's work during the war did achieve wage parity with men. One such was Edith Kent, the first woman to work as a welder in Devonport dockyard in Plymouth, where she began work in 1941. In 1943, a skilled worker short enough, at 4 ft 11 in, to crawl inside the torpedo tubes she worked on, she was given a pay rise from £5 6s (five pounds six shillings) to £6 6s, which meant she was earning the same as the men, and more than some of them. At this time, the average male manual worker in Britain was earning about £5 8s 6d a week. The hard work did Edith Kent no harm. She celebrated her hundredth birthday with a tea dance in 2008.

eighty hours a week, and even, in aircraft factories when the very survival of the nation depended on having enough planes to fight the enemy, an exhausting 112 hours a week. In fact, forty-five hours was more usual, in eight-hour shifts if the factory was on a twenty-four-hour production schedule, and up to twelve-hour shifts – say, from 6 a.m. to 6 p.m. – if the factory or works did not carry on through the night. If a woman was married and had a husband at home, she might not see him for days on end, if one or other of them was on the night shift (from 10 p.m. until 6 a.m.). A lot of young married women chose pregnancy as the way out of full-time factory work.

When piece-work was brought in, replacing an earlier system which provided bonuses for those who worked well or exceeded targets, it was very easy for a woman not to earn her full wage, perhaps by having to wait for a broken machine to be repaired. During the war, equal pay for equal work did not become a target for women as it was to do in the decades after it. On the whole, most women were happy to be getting money regularly, which could be used to help with household bills. Even when they were in better paid jobs – generally to be found in munitions work or in transport, especially the railways or buses – women expected to be paid less than men.

Another group of women doing men's work during the war were the members of the Women's Land Army. Armies of female land workers were set up in Scotland and in England/Wales during World War I, but were rather too late on the scene to be really effective. With war obviously looming again, the lesson was learnt and the Women's Land Army (WLA) was reconvened in June 1939, with an official minimum recruitment age of seventeen – which was often ignored or lied about by girls eager to join. By 1944, the WLA was a force of eighty thousand women, a third of whom came from Britain's cities and had no previous experience of farm work. A sister organisation, the Women's Timber Corps, one of whose more vital wartime jobs was cutting pit props for coal mines, was started in 1942 and eventually numbered six thousand women.

Although Land Girls, and the Lumberjills of the Timber Corps, were issued with a uniform, including a green jersey, cream shirt, brown breeches, brown felt hat and khaki overcoat, the term 'Army' was something of a misnomer, even though the WLA was definitely in the front line of the 'Dig for Victory' campaign. A Land Girl could modify her uniform to suit her personal taste – the breeches, although at first seen as quite daring style-wise, were often replaced by dungarees or standard trousers – and the only discipline she was subjected to was the threat of dismissal if her work was not up to standard. Since dismissal from the WLA simply meant redirection into the auxiliary services or war industry, deliberately trying to get the sack was not much of an option for exhausted Land Girls or Lumberjills.

▶ *LAND ARMY GIRLS*
A pair of Women's Land Army volunteers take a welcome break to drink from Lady Well, Sticklepath, England. The sign on the well reads 'Lady Well. Drink and Be Thankful.'

Many young women chose to join the WLA because they thought working out-of-doors was preferable to being cooped up in a factory and also, since they would be in the country, they would be far away from the bombing. On the whole, the Women's Land Army met both these criteria – although not always: the artist Mary Fedden found herself, after just six weeks at an agricultural college in Devon, working on a farm in Gloucestershire next to the Filton aircraft works which was subjected to very regular bombings for a year. And it was often exhausting work, with, all too often, very basic accommodation without hot water or electricity to look forward to at the end of the working day. Nor was the pay very good: about 17s 6d (about 82p) a week, plus keep.

In fact, being a Land Girl was far more arduous than working in a factory. The work had to be done every day, and sometimes far into the night, summer and winter, in good weather and bad. On many farms, there might be one or two older male farm workers to advise and help with really heavy work, like building hay ricks or pig pens, but many Land Girls found themselves on an all-female farm, where they were the farmer's only help, with perhaps some help from schoolboys and schoolgirls at harvest time and also some help, later in the war, from German and Italian prisoners of war. Many Land Girls found that German POWs worked harder than the Italians, but that the latter were much more light-hearted, and sang a lot – beautifully.

More than sixty years after World War II ended, Britain officially honoured the work of the Women's Land Army, which was disbanded in 1950. There were still some thirty

TUPPENCE A TAIL

The rat population of Britain in 1940 was estimated to be fifty million, with large numbers of them in agricultural areas. The Women's Land Army included about a thousand Land Girls trained to specialise in rat-catching, an essential task in farm barns, sheds and outhouses. The work included the correct mixing and use of rat poison and how to smoke rats out of their nests.

Because the Land Girls' wages were not large, many girls, specialised in the job or not, joined rat-catching sessions with the farmer and his dogs in order to earn a little extra cash. The standard price for rat skins was 2d a tail. Another source of income was moleskins. The moles, when killed, would be skinned and the pelts mounted on boards to dry before being sold.

▲ *LEAPING LANDGIRLS*
At the end of a hard day's work these two land girls leap with joy on a farm somewhere in Surrey.

thousand surviving Land Girls and Timberjills in 2008, all of them eligible to receive a special commemorative badge, to be worn on Remembrance Sundays and other official occasions, recognising their 'tireless work for the benefit of their nation' in wartime.

Nursing provided a third alternative for women choosing to do civilian work during the war. War made huge demands on Britain's civilian nursing systems, severely aggravated by the fact that the second world war, unlike the first, was fought as much on the Home Front as on the battlefield. Trained nurses were needed in Britain as much at ARP first-aid posts, in ambulances and in air-raid shelters as they were in hospitals, which themselves had thousands more patients to deal with than in peace-time. While teaching hospitals could train their own nurses, other organisations, including the British Red Cross, the Order of St John of Jerusalem, the First Air Nursing Yeomanry and the Voluntary Aid Detachments (VADs), were called on to provide nurses both at home and overseas, many of them in the auxiliary services, where they worked as volunteers rather than service personnel.

The Ministry of Health set up an Emergency Medical Service before the war started and also began recalling trained nurses who had retired or who had left nursing when they married. There was also the Civil Nursing reserve, which young women could join on a part-time basis; the advent of war turned Civil Nursing reservists into auxiliary nurses, liable to be called up to help with the various evacuation schemes that were quickly put into action.

By the end of September 1939, the Ministry had enrolled fifteen thousand trained nurses and twenty thousand auxiliary nurses and accepted for training another seventy-six thousand people, most of them women. By the end of the war, so great was the need for trained nurses, that the training time for State Registered Nurses had been reduced by 1945 from four years to three. Since the minimum age for training was eighteen, many girls younger than this did part-time training, joining organisations such as the Red Cross and working in emergency centres for the homeless or first aid posts as well as in hospitals.

The biggest provider of nurse aides during the war was the Voluntary Aid Detachment (VAD). Formed in 1910, the VAD, most of whose members were women and all of whom were volunteers, did invaluable work, both at home, on the Western Front and even further afield during World War I. Before World War II broke out, VADs were reorganised so that they could give additional support to the general medical services in the event of war.

About fifteen thousand women became VADs during the war, many of them by joining the Red Cross, which gave them some initial nurse-aid training; VADs were civilian volunteers, although they did wear a smart uniform, and were not counted as part of the auxiliary services, even when working in services hospitals or medical centres. As untrained volunteers, VADs tended to get all the dirty work but also found themselves doing the work of qualified nurses, such as giving injections and helping in operations.

▲ *VOLUNTARY AID DETACHMENT*
Nurses demonstrating how to fit an infant's gas helmet at the VAD annual training camp in Fleetwood. It was fitted with a hand-operated pump underneath for supplying air to the child.

DEFENDING THE PEOPLE

British towns were bombed from aeroplanes during World War I – not extensively and with less than fifteen thousand people killed, but enough to bring anti-aircraft guns, air-raid warnings and searchlights into use as part of the nation's regular home defence equipment. It was clear that should there be another war, the British population would be in the front line. Clear, too, was the fact that Britain's citizens would have to be involved in a radically improved civil defence operation, expanded to include defending the nation from air attack.

Although the British government began thinking about air raid precautions in 1924, during the meetings of a sub-committee of the Committee for Imperial Defence, not a lot in the way of serious planning was done for another decade. A committee set up in 1931 to look into the provision of Air Raid Precautions (ARP) services in London reported that, in the face of some truly appalling estimates of the number of bombs that could be expected to drop on Britain from the first day of any war, plans should be made to evacuate about 3.5 million people from London.

In 1934-5 ARP planning was extended beyond London to cover the country as a whole, as part of the nation's overall civil defence planning; at the same time, an Air Raid Precautions department was formed within the Home Office. ARP planners were jerked into more serious action by the part played by planes in the Spanish Civil War from 1936, especially the hugely destructive bombing in April 1937 of the Basque town of Guernica by the German Condor Legion supporting the Fascists. In France, the government had already issued a handbook explaining its evacuation plans to all French people.

At first, the action in Britain was still moderate – not much more than a radio appeal in January 1937 for volunteers for ARP work and a request to local authorities to beef up their civil defence planning, in which ARP would play a major role. The response was poor, and at the beginning of 1938 the government used force, in the form of the Air Raid Precautions Act, to get local authorities to do detailed planning on civil defence, including how the ARP, first aid and ambulance, and fire services and bomb disposal units would be organised and used in the event of war. Interestingly, Civil defence did not become an organisation with capital letters – Civil Defence – until September 1941, when Air Raid Precautions and the new National Fire Service, (NFS), were amalgamated. The Home Guard was another important element of wartime civil defence.

Each local authority was directed to have a Civil Defence headquarters building, from which the various services would be directed to where their services were needed most. The London Regional Civil Defence

▲ *EVACUATION REHEARSAL*
A group of children set off on an evacuation rehearsal in London.

Headquarters, which oversaw the work of the nine civil defence areas into which the capital was divided, was set up in a hastily reinforced basement in the Geological Museum in South Kensington. When the first workers – all of them young women aged nineteen or twenty – arrived, there was still plenty of evidence of the presence of rats and mice amid the cement dust left behind by the reinforcing work. The women worked in shifts – ten or twelve women in each of three eight-hour shifts every day, with the first shift starting at 7 a.m. and the last at 11 p.m.

Volunteering for ARP remained slow until Hitler invaded Czechoslovakia in

A RAIN OF DEATH

The 1931 committee looking into ARP services in Britain was given a terrifying series of estimates by experts. The committee was told that in a future war, the country could expect to receive an opening assault from the enemy's air force (aka Germany's Luftwaffe) of up to 3500 tons of bombs in the first 24 hours, and as many as 600 tons of bombs dropped on it every day thereafter. In the opening assault, there could be 60,000 people killed and 120,000 wounded; in every week after that, the ARP services could be dealing with 66,000 dead and 130,000 wounded. In the face of such figures, the committee was forced to the conclusion that evacuation would be an essential part of wartime defence. No one seemed to have doubted the ability of Germany to produce bombers in such huge numbers and of a size necessary to deliver such attacks. In the event, such cataclysmic figures were never realised. Over the 76 nights of bombing during the Blitz in London there were nearly 10,000 deaths and at the end of the devastating eleven-hour raid on Coventry on 14 November 1940, 554 people were dead and a thousand houses had been destroyed, along with many factories and Coventry's medieval cathedral.

September 1938. Now volunteer numbers soared, with the new members finding themselves helping with ARP blackout trials and practice responses to 'incidents' – ARP volunteers always responded to 'incidents', never to fires, gas-main explosions, burst water-mains or bombs.

The ARP jobs that men and women could volunteer for included wardens and messengers, casualty and first aid workers, stretcher bearers, ambulance drivers and people trained to provide an anti-gas service. From the first, women volunteered in greater numbers than men, perhaps because men knew that in the event of war they would either be in reserved occupations at home or called-up into the forces. It was not until May 1940 that men were given their own civil defence organisation, the Local Defence Volunteers, later re-named the Home Guard and soon known to all as 'Dad's Army'.

Women who volunteered early for the ARP services were mostly directed into the ambulance services, either as drivers or as first aid assistants. As civilian volunteers, they had no ranks or officer titles, but there was an ARP uniform. At first, this simply amounted to the ARP volunteer wearing a

▲ *COVENTRY CATHEDRAL*
The ruins of Coventry Cathedral after bombing by Germans during WWII.

▲ *BOMB DAMAGE*
An air raid warden clambers through the ruins of a building after a World War II air raid on London.

Sterling silver ARP badge

metal helmet, an armband, a metal badge and carrying a whistle. By the end of 1939, ARP women were wearing mackintosh-style coats made of a thin, dark-blue denim-like material. A much more practical heavier battle-dress style uniform, including trousers, greatcoat and beret was introduced in 1941. Eventually, ARP people who had completed their training were given a fine sterling silver badge, designed by Eric Gill, the sculptor and type designer produced by the Royal Mint and issued by the Government. As local authorities issued their own Civil Defence badges, there was soon a great number of Civil Defence and ARP badges to be seen on the lapels and caps of ARP workers throughout the country.

Women who had volunteered to be air raid wardens when war was declared, found themselves with little to do in the first months of the war except avoid accidents in blacked-out streets. As Helen Brook, who founded the Brook Advisory Centres in the 1960s, recalled, she would often have to get out of bed at 2 a.m., 'dressed up in all this

1942

MAY
- USA surrenders Philippines to Japan.
- The US Congress establishes the Women's Auxiliary Army Corps (WAAC).
- Petrol rationing starts in the US. Nationwide rationing to start in September.
- Britain abandons Burma to Japan.
- Mexico declares war on Germany and Italy.
- Britain's Royal Air Force commences its 1000-bomber attack on German industrial targets.

JUNE
- US Navy defeats the Japanese in the Midway Battle.
- Roosevelt authorises a project to develop an atomic bomb.
- German field marshal Rommel and his troops capture Tobruk in Libya.
- Germany invades Egypt.
- The FBI captures eight German agents who have landed by U-boat on Long Island.

JULY
- French police round up 30,000 Jews and German troops transport them to concentration camps. Only about thirty survive.
- Jews are deported from Warsaw to the Treblinka concentration camp.
- Women being accepted for Volutary Emergency Services (WAVES) is authorised by US Congress.

AUGUST
- Canadian commando troops attack Dieppe.
- The Battle of Stalingrad begins.
- Brazil declares war on Germany and Italy.

SEPTEMBER
- Germany lays siege to Stalingrad.
- Women's Airforce Service Pilots (WASPs) are established in the US.

CALLING FOR A MILLION VOLUNTEERS

'If the emergency arose, I know you would come in your hundreds of thousands. But you would be untrained. For the work we may have to do one man trained beforehand is worth two or three who come at the last moment. We want at least a million men and women, and we want them for work that in an emergency would be exacting and dangerous. The job is not an amusement in peace time, nor would it be a soft job in time of war. It is a serious job for free men and women who care for their fellows and their Country.' With these words, reprinted in a recruitment leaflet issued by the Home Office and the Scottish Office, the Home Secretary, in a wireless broadcast concerning the Air Raid Precautions Act in March 1938, launched the recruitment drive for British citizens to take their part 'in the voluntary organisation of the Air Raid Precautions Services'.

gear', which included trousers so long they had to be rolled up, a whistle, a rattle and a tin hat, and walk about the pitch-black streets of her beat, north of Oxford Street in London, for two hours. Her refuge, should bombs drop, was the area steps down to a cellar. Her 'boss' was a retired naval commander who made his wardens keep naval hours and have dog watches.

The Phoney War came to an end amidst rumours of invasion and German spies everywhere. As Virginia Woolf noted in her diary in May 1940, 'Rodmell [the local village] burns with rumours. Are we to be bombed, evacuated? Guns that shake the windows. Hospital ships sunk. So it comes our way. Today's rumour is the nun in the bus who pays her fare with a man's hand.' Then

Germany invaded Norway, the Belgians capitulated, and the British Expeditionary Force and thousands of French soldiers found themselves at Dunkirk, with their backs to the sea.

With the Phoney War finished, it was time for the girls in the London Regional Civil Defence headquarters to put away their knitting, reading and table tennis. Now, in properly bombproof quarters, the head-quarters staff were fully occupied manning its telephone exchange, message room and control room, from where they coordinated the ARP, ambulance, fire and rescue services in London.

As the reality of the war sunk in, so did the reality of being a volunteer ARP worker, which had suddenly become a much more

▲ *ARP POSTER*
One of a series of British government recruitment posters for the ARP (Air Raid Precautions)
encouraging women to do their part for the war effort.

▲ *SALT OF THE EARTH*
Nurses waiting on dock for wounded soldiers to be unloaded from a British hospital ship.

serious and dangerous role. Over the subsequent months more and more men were called up for service, so women played an increasingly vital part in ARP, as wardens, ambulance drivers (with knowledge of elementary mechanics), fire-watchers, auxiliary nurses, gas decontamination experts (for which they had to have a certificate confirming that they had completed a special training course), motorcycle messengers, and directing the responses to 'incidents'.

At the height of the Blitz in London in 1940, one in every six ARP Wardens, the key to calm, efficient local civil defence, was a woman. Their posts were concrete boxes, measuring 10 feet x 8 feet, and protected by sandbags piled up round them and on their roofs.

Another Civil Defence service in which women played a large part was the Auxiliary Fire Service (AFS). This was a voluntary organisation, founded in 1938 and originally aimed at men only, which was intended to supplement the work of the London Fire Brigade and the country's local fire service organisations, of which there were 1600 in 1939. By the time the war started, some twenty-three thousand men and women had volunteered for the AFS, the women getting in by virtue of a rather vague clause in the

▼ *FIRE TRAINING*
Chorus girls who responded to the call for volunteer fire watchers being trained by Newcastle fire brigade to deal with incendiary devices on the roof of Newcastle Theatre Royal.

WOMEN'S WAGES IN CIVIL DEFENCE

In all areas of working life in Britain in the 1940s, women were generally paid less than men, even when doing the same work. When women teachers asked for pay parity with men during the war, Prime Minister Winston Churchill snorted that their demand was 'impertinent'. As in all work in wartime Britain, so in Civil Defence work, women were generally paid considerably less than men. In autumn 1940, in the early days of the Blitz, full-time ARP and AFS male workers were being paid a wage of £3 5s a week; women were getting £2 3s 6d – a third less. Some part-time male workers, who might be losing money because of working fewer hours in their day job, got compensation of a few shillings a day. Women did not.

Government's 'National Service' booklet that said that women 'between the ages of twenty and fifty' would be wanted for 'appropriate services'.

At first, 'appropriate services' for women in the AFS meant mainly administrative work in fire stations and civil defence control centres, where they did such typical women's work as operating telephone switchboards, doing clerical work and running mobile canteens. But before long, as elsewhere in wartime Britain, women were doing men's work, driving fire tenders and messengers' motorbikes (which they repaired and maintained) and working as pump teams and fire-hose operators.

Soon there were so many all-women pump teams in the AFS that women-only competitions were held. When Mrs Marjorie Meath's team from D Division HQ in Birmingham won the cup in the Midlands women's teams competition, the cup was taken round the eleven stations in the division – and was filled with an appropriately celebratory liquid at each one. There was at least one fire station in Britain – Holcombe Fire Station in Chatham, Kent – that was operated entirely by women. Twenty-five women members of the AFS were killed on duty during the war, and many more were hurt.

The AFS played a major part in fighting the fires of the Blitz in London and other cities in 1940–1. Often, relations between the auxiliaries and the fire-fighting professionals were strained, not just over fire-fighting matters but also – and more often – over questions of pay and working conditions,

▲ *AT THE DOUBLE*
Members of the First Aid Nursing Yeomanry (FANYS) running to their ambulances during a 'stand to' in the Southern Command during World War II.

with the auxiliaries, 'doing their bit for the war effort', being ready to accept low wages, no overtime, no holiday pay and, often, no uniform; much more often problems arose because of the widely varying sizes of equipment, especially hoses, used in different local fire services, so sending reinforcements across county boundaries was often a waste of manpower. In August 1941, the National Fire Service was formed by merging the country's professional fire-fighting bodies and the AFS.

Women were given their own ranking structure within the fire service. By 1943, the most senior female rank was Chief Woman Fire Officer, epaulettes with three silver stripes alternating with red and topped by a small impeller signifying her rank. Below her came Regional Woman Fire Officer, then Area Officer, Assistant Area Officer, Group Officer, Assistant Group Officer and Leading Firewoman.

It should not be forgotten that during the war, fire-fighting, particularly dealing with incendiary bombs, became a civil defence job that many people did in addition to their daily work. From September 1940, when the first Fire Watchers Order was issued, it was compulsory for men to do a minimum of forty-eight hours fire-watching duty every

1942

OCTOBER
- Germany carries out a mass execution of Jews at the Mizocz ghetto, Ukraine.
- Hitler orders the execution of all captured British commandos.

NOVEMBER
- Under General Eisenhower, a joint US–British force of 400,000 troops begins landing at Casablanca, Oran and Algiers. They successfully overpower the French garrisons there.
- Mahatma Ghandi demands independence from Britain for India. Churchill responds by saying:
  'I have not become the King's First Minister in order to preside over the liquidation of the British Empire!'
- The Naval Battle of Guadalcanal between Japanese and American forces begins near Guadalcanal. It lasts for three days.
- Aviators from the USS *Enterprise* sink the Japanese heavy cruiser *BB- Hiei*.

DECEMBER
- Manhattan Project – A team led by Enrico Fermi initiates the first self-sustaining nuclear chain reaction.
- Coffee joins the list of rationed items in the USA.

- The first surface-to-surface guided missile is launched in Peenemünde. It was designed by thirty-year-old rocket engineer Wernher von Braun.
- SS Chief Heinrich Himmler (*left*) orders that the Roma (gypsy) people be sent to Auschwitz for extermination.

month; as with most things in wartime, women also found themselves doing fire-watching duty, usually in their own work places.

All work places in the danger areas, from banks and offices to department stores, shops and factories, churches and cinemas instituted rotas for their staff and other helpers to do fire-watching duty at night. Fire-watchers were usually given some instruction in dealing with incendiary bombs and operating stirrup pumps. It was the men and women who worked in St Paul's Cathedral in London who did most of the work of dealing with the incendiary bombs on the building's roof, so that its great dome was able to rise unscathed and apparently invincible above the flames and smoke of the Blitz.

While ARP and the AFS/NFS could count large numbers of women in their volunteer forces, there were other, smaller all-women volunteer organisations that did invaluable work during the war. One was the Women's Auxiliary Police Force. Never numbering more than ten thousand, the force did mostly administrative and driving work and was attached to county and city police forces. Although it never became a national force, the WAPF did have its own insignia and uniform.

Another civil defence organisation for women was the Civil Nursing Reserve. This was a voluntary organisation that trained assistant nurses and which, after 1940, was augmented by Red Cross and St John Ambulance nurses.

While Britain's governing powers may have been slow to come round to the idea that women could do men's work in wartime, they never, unlike their counterparts in the Soviet Union, came to terms with the idea that women could

▲ *POLICE DRIVER*
A member of the Women's Auxiliary Police Corps helps the war effort by driving an ambulance.

shoulder arms like their fathers and brothers in the defence of their country. The suggestion from women that they might be allowed to join the Home Guard was rejected by the government in 1940, and the increasingly vocal demand from such feminist women Members of Parliament as Lady Astor, Dr Irene Ward and Dr Edith Summerskill that women should be allowed to serve their country fully in the armed services was never considered.

In response to this, the redoubtable Dr Summerskill, MP for Fulham West in London, thinking that it was wrong that in wartime with invasion threatening, half the adult population did not know at least how to use a rifle, started the Women's Home Defence League (WHDL) in 1941. Dr Summerskill did not see the members of the WHDL replacing the men of the Home Guard; rather, they could be of great help to them, doing less physically demanding work that would free the men for active anti-enemy work.

Within a year, some two hundred local units of the WHDL had been set up in all parts of the country. Members, who wore a badge but not a uniform, learned such suitably womanly things as first aid, field cooking and Morse code. They were also given training in unarmed combat and the use of a .22 rifle. The cash to fund such training was raised through a wide range of social activities. By April 1943 the government had backed down sufficiently to permit the members of the WHDL to join the Home Guard as 'nominated women'; in July 1944, the 'nominated women' were renamed Home Guard Auxiliaries. At war's end, there were thirty thousand of them.

▲ *LADY ASTOR*
American-born Nancy Langhorne Astor (1879–1964) became the first woman to serve as a member of the British Parliament, a position she held from 1919 to 1945.

▶ *HOME GUARDS*
Two women participating in a civilian defence drill during World War II, after being allowed to join the Home Guard as 'nominated women' in July 1944.

INTO THE ARMED FORCES

The Military Training Act that came into force in Britain in May 1939 introduced conscription – but only for young men aged twenty and twenty-one. It did not apply to women. Nor did the National Service (Armed Forces) Act, which Parliament passed on the first day of war and which brought in the possibility of conscription for men aged between eighteen and forty-one (unless they were in a Reserved Occupation, a list of which had been published back in November 1938).

▲ *HANDLING A RIFLE*
A WRNS officer learning how to handle a rifle during her training as an armourer.

In 1939 women could volunteer to work in the armed forces from the age of seventeen, in one of the auxiliary arms of the three main services – the Auxiliary Territorial Service (ATS) for the army, the Women's Auxiliary Air Force (WAAF) for the Royal Air Force, and the Women's Royal Navy

▲ *WRNS MECHANICS*
Although initially recruited to release men to serve at sea, the women of the WRNS soon took on a diverse range of work that had been previously considered beyond their capabilities. Here two members can be seen servicing a plane.

THE ATS SECRETARY AND THE END OF THE WAR

The last posting of the war for ATS sergeant secretary Susan Heald was at the Supreme Headquarters Allied Expeditionary Force in Rheims. For five days in May 1945 she and other typists typed surrender documents to be signed by Germany from early in the morning until late at night. Working on old Imperial typewriters, Sergeant Heald typed up the English and German versions of the Act of Military Surrender and its many attachments, while other typists prepared Russian and French versions. Sergeant Heald witnessed the signing of the surrender documents by Germany's chief of staff, General Alfred Jodl, on 7 May. She then typed out the signal to the War Office in London that said 'The mission of this Allied Force was fulfilled at 0241, local time, May 7th, 1945'. She and the other typists celebrated by drinking champagne out of mess tins – and then went to bed, as they had been working non-stop for twenty hours. Sergeant Heald was mentioned in despatches for her work.

Service (WRNS) for the Royal Navy. There was no thought at this time of sending women into combat; rather their role in the auxiliary services was seen as doing work of an administrative, secretarial and catering nature, thus freeing up men for fighting work on the field of battle.

Even before the start of World War II, young women had volunteered with enthusiasm for the auxiliary services, many of them because they wanted to emulate fathers and brothers in the way they served their country in its hour of need in World War I, but many because they fancied the idea of getting away from home, travelling, finding adventure and wearing a smart uniform. It was probably from among the latter that the drift away from the auxiliary services gathered pace during the Phoney War. At this time in the ATS, for instance, there were only five 'trades' offered women, and none of which were exciting or adventurous.

It was partly to counter this loss of female personnel in the services that the government made the women's auxiliary services officially part of the Armed Forces of the Crown in April 1941, following this up in the July of that year by giving women full military status – the natural corollary of which was that women were now subject to full military discipline.

When the conscription of women was introduced in Britain, in December 1941, by way of the National Service (No. 2) Act, it

◀ *NOTHING STOPS FOR WAR*
Joan Harcourt was the continuity girl at the film studios where they filmed Kipps. *She had to continue to work during an air raid but was given a tin hat as protection.*

1943

JANUARY
- The USA and Britain give up territorial rights in China.
- The first uprising of Jews in the Warsaw ghettos.
- Nazi doctor Josef Mengele starts experimenting on twins at Auschwitz concentration camp.
- Churchill and Roosevelt hold a conference at Casablanca in Morocco.
- Duke Ellington plays his first concern at New York's Carnegie Hall.
- The main German forces in Stalingrad surrender to the Soviet Union.
- Fifty bombers mount the first entirely US air raid against Germany.
- British forces capture Tripoli.

FEBRUARY
- The last Nazi forces surrender to the Soviets following the Battle of Stalingrad.
- Allied forces capture Guadalcanal after heavy fighting.
- German General Erwin Rommel and his troops launch an offensive against Allied defences in Tunisia.
- Joseph Goebbels delivers his famous Sportpalast speech.
- General Hideki Tojo becomes military dictator of Japan.
- A group of wives of Jewish men gather in Berlin to stop the deportation of their men to concentration camps. They eventually succeeded in forcing Goebbels to release 1500 men.
- Russia bombs Sweden and Finland.

MARCH
- 173 people are killed in their rush to try and get into an air raid shelter in Bethnal Green tube station in London.

▲ *WHEELING A TORPEDO*
Members of the WRNS wheeling a torpedo for
loading onto a Swordfish warplane.

▶ *ANY OLD COOKING*
ATS recruits were taught how to set up and run
an emergency field kitchen. The kitchen could
be built from dustbins, milk churns and other
items of everyday life.

applied only to unmarried women between
the ages of twenty and thirty; nineteen-
year-olds were brought into conscription
range in 1942. The Act did not force women
to take on 'combatant duties' if they chose to
join one of the women's auxiliary services,
or to handle a lethal weapon unless they
were willing to do so. Women began
receiving their call-up papers in March 1942
and could choose to be 'directed' towards

work in industry or the civil defences or to be conscripted into the armed forces. By the summer of 1944, some 467,000 women had chosen to go into the auxiliary services.

The ATS, which was begun on a voluntary basis in 1938, attracted the largest number of women – more than 210,000 when it was at its peak strength in mid-1943 and by the time the war ended they were doing men's work in more than eighty trades, most of them in the 'skilled' category. Less than a quarter of women in the ATS worked as cooks, domestic workers or clerks and

another 10 per cent or so were telephonists and teleprinter operators.

When writer, broadcaster and actor Anne Valery joined the ATS at seventeen, she found basic training 'a doddle' compared with the austere and regimented life of a girls' public school. 'And', she wrote in *Talking About the War*, 'it had the added bonus of no compulsory cold baths, evenings off in the fleshpots of wherever I was stationed, plus the heady freedom of unsupervised leaves.... For girls from poor families, army life was an undreamt luxury

▲ *WOMEN MECHANICS*
As the need for trained men increased, members of the Women's Division could be found carrying out everything from aircraft and car mechanics, to packing parachutes and ferrying aircraft between airfields. These women are rivetting inside an aircraft fusilage.

because of its three meals a day, a change of underclothes, new shoes, and nightwear instead of a vest. Many had never been to the dentist and their teeth were in such a bad state that our camp dentist told me that sometimes he had to spend an entire session cleaning them, before he could see what needed to be done.... Grouped round a smelly stove in the barrack room, ex-debs, orphans and secretaries swapped their life stories....By the end of Basic Training, class had all but disappeared.'

For many ATS women, including George VI's daughter, Princess Elizabeth, their work took them into the engine, under the chassis and into the driving seat of a vast array of army vehicles, from staff cars, military ambulances and three-ton trucks to gun limbers and tanks. They were trained in essential vehicle maintenance at ATS Motor Transport Training Centres. In 1943 it was estimated that 80 per cent of Army driving was done by women. By this time ATS members were also serving with regular army units in anti-aircraft batteries, usually acting as spotters for the men who manned the guns, and working with the Home Guard as well.

When the ATS was first established it provided support to the RAF, but in 1939 the WAAF was formed and took over the ATS's role. Like the ATS, the WAAF grew rapidly after the war began, counting more than sixty-four thousand officers and other ranks by 1940, 182,000 at the end of the war. Their duties remained firmly on the ground, however, where the majority of them eventually replaced airmen working in over eighty different trades, including aircraft maintenance and instrument and flight mechanics. WAAF women became skilled electricians, fitters and armourers. Other airwomen worked as drivers, clerks or cooks, and a few ran classes instructing the Home Guard in aircraft recognition.

Particularly vital roles played by airwomen in wartime were the interpretation of photographs of enemy targets, including airfields, industrial sites and supply stores, the plotting of incoming waves of enemy aircraft, and meteorological observation. They also took the operation of barrage balloons over from the RAF.

By 1944 most of the Service Meteorological Officers in the Flying Training Command were women; their work was very important, given the way in which weather conditions could affect the success or failure of bombing missions. A WAAF meteorological observer had to make hourly observations of the weather, sending her findings by teleprinter to group headquarters, and drawing up weather maps. She often found herself working at night when the rest of her

We service that men may fly.
The motto of the Royal Canadia Air Force Women's Division.

KEEPING THE BALLOONS FLYING

Barrage balloons, or 'blimps' as they came to be called, were flown from open spaces over cities, ports and harbours, airfields, industrial sites and other places to discourage low-level attacks and dive-bombing. They were initially operated by ten-man crews of the RAF's Balloon Command, but in early 1941 were gradually handed over to the WAAF, with sixteen airwomen doing the job of the ten RAF men. Eventually, the WAAF operated 1029 barrage balloon sites throughout Britain. It was hard, physically demanding and dangerous work, especially when there were strong winds blowing. The important things about the balloons was not the balloons themselves so much as the steel cables – lethal to aircraft – that the balloons held upright in the air.

▲ *AMY JOHNSON*
English aviator Amy Johnson (1903–1941) standing in front of her Gipsy Moth just before
she undertook a nineteen day solo flight to Australia on 5 May 1930.

station's Met Office staff were quietly sleeping, waiting for that night's mission to return home.

As WAAF personnel were not permitted to fly planes, any woman wanting to do so had to forget about the WAAF and try for a place in the civilian Air Transport Auxiliary (ATA). The ATA was founded in September 1939 to provide an aircraft ferrying service, generally from factory to airfield, that would not use valuable RAF pilots. It began by recruiting men only – of course – who had pilots licences and at least 250 hours' flying experience. As in all other areas of the war, however, recruitment policy soon changed and from January 1940 women with more

than 600 hours flying experience were recruited by an initially reluctant ATA.

At first they were not allowed to fly operational aircraft or to fly outside Britain, nor were they ever attached to RAF units, remaining in their own civilian pools. Eventually 164 women, including the near-legendary Amy Johnson and Diana Barnato, daughter of the motor-racing champion Woolf Barnato, as well as Americans, Australians, South Africans and others from a total of twenty-eight nations, were recruited into the ATA, 108 of them as pilots.

Once they were permitted to fly operational aircraft – mostly Hurricanes, Mosquitoes and, their favourite, Spitfires –

SECRETIVE WOMEN

While British Intelligence was not a branch of the armed forces, its work brought it into very close contact with them. No one knows exactly how many men and women were involved in the work of the Special Operations Executive (SOE), but there are thought to have been some 10,000 men and 3,200 women working for the SOE in 1944, when it was at its greatest operational strength. Of the more than 400 agents sent to France by the SOE, thirty-nine were women, thirteen of whom never made it back to Britain and safety. Three SOE women agents – Noor Inayat

Khan, Odette Hallowes and Violette Szabo – were awarded the George Cross. As for that other arm of British Intelligence, Bletchley Park, as Winston Church remarked, they were 'the geese that laid golden eggs, but never cackled', so the numbers of women working there have not been confirmed. A few women were at Bletchley Park from the time the Secret Intelligence Service moved in briefly during the Munich Crisis and then permanently in autumn 1939. Their numbers increased in 1940, when several of them worked as section heads.

▲ *PILOTS ADJUST CHUTES*
Women pilots of the Air Transport Auxiliary (ATA) adjusting their parachutes. From 1941, the ATA took on the roles of Royal Air Force ferry pools transporting aircraft between factories, airfields and maintenance units.

▲ *CABINET EXCHANGE*
The telephone exchange in the Cabinet War Rooms were situated under Whitehall. The exchange
was housed in a reinforced bunker to protect it from attack during the Blitz.

they spent the war ferrying combat planes from the factories to RAF squadrons, Fleet Air Arm bases and the maintenance depots. As Diana Barnato recalled later, they flew every day in all weathers, without radio and unarmed, avoiding barrage balloons and occasionally being shot at by the enemy and, 'now and then, by our own side.' Later in the war they flew aircraft to squadrons in Europe, including France and the Netherlands. They were the only women of the war's Western partners who flew in a war

zone. Even the women of the US Women's Air Service Pilots (WASPs) were kept at least three thousand miles from a war zone.

An organisation which attracted women who wished to be drivers, to bear arms and to be connected to the Army, although not in it, was the First Aid Nursing Yeomanry, or FANY, an organisation set up in World War I, during which FANYs soon stopped being mounted on horses and took to driving vehicles. During World War II the FANY developed a strong link with the Special

Operations Executive (SOE), the secret intelligence organisation founded, on a direct order from Churchill, in 1940. The women agents working for the SOE were drawn from the ranks of the FANY and the WAAF, and FANYs provided drivers, despatch riders, coders, wireless operators – their most essential function – and even parachute packers for the SOE.

The third important women's auxiliary force was the Women's Royal Navy Service (WRNS), whose members were invariably called 'Wrens'. The closest that Wrens got to sea was manning harbour craft in all weathers in naval bases all round Britain's coast. They were never allowed to go to sea in a ship of the Royal Navy; as a wartime recruiting poster put it, 'Join the Wrens and free a man for the Fleet'.

The Wrens' greatest task during the war was plotting the progress, day and night, of the Battle of the Atlantic from the

▲ WOMEN ON WATCH
Women members of the ATS operating a searchlight during a period of surveillance.

Operations Room of Western Approaches Command and their often most dangerous one was serving as coastal mine-spotters. If a Wren was a Visual Signaller, she spent much of her time outside in all weathers keeping contact with ships at anchor, outside the harbour where she was based, by means of Morse code, semaphore, flag signals and Aldis signalling lamps, all of which she had to use competently and efficiently.

By 1944 two-thirds of WRNS officers were doing the work of naval officers who had been sent to sea, replacing many of them as cypher decoders and in technical and secretarial work. As in the other women's auxiliary services, there were also many 'trades' undertaken by WRNSs, from welders and carpenters to armourers and ship repair and maintenance workers.

For the women who served in the

SEMAPHORE

One of the more common methods of communication by Signal men and women during World War II was the use of Semaphore. Semaphore is the communication between ships using a flag alphabet. The signalman or woman on a ship used hand-held flags to send messages to nearby ships. They held a flag in each hand and then rotated the flags into certain positions, each one representing a

different letter of the alphabet.

The semaphore signalling system was designed by the Chappe brothers in France in the late 18th century. It was originally used to carry despatches between French army units, including those commanded by Napoleon. Today the flags used are usually square and divided diagonally into a red and a yellow section, with the red in the uppermost triangle.

▲ *JOBS FOR WOMEN*
A woman learns how to use an LNER telegraph machine during World War II. The machine is used for transmitting and receiving messages over long distances.

1943

MARCH *continued ...*

- First flight of Gloster Meteor jet in Britain.
- German U-boats sink 108 ships this month.
- Germany invades Hungary.
- Meat rationing begins in the USA. The ration is 28 ounces per week.
- German forces liquidate the Jewish ghetto at Kraków.

APRIL

- Bolivia declares war on Germany and Italy.
- 16,000 POWs and 80,000 Asian slave labourers die during the construction of a Japanese railway between Thailand and Burma (up until June 1944).
- In the USA all meat, fats, canned goods and cheese are now rationed. In an attempt to stop inflation, Roosevelt freezes wages and prices.

MAY

- German troops surrender to the Soviet Union in the Crimea.
- German and Italian troops surrender to Britain in North Africa.
- German troops destroy the Warsaw ghetto.
- The USA and Britain manage to destroy 30 per cent of Germany's U-boats this month.
- The Dambuster Raids by RAF 617 Squadron on German dams.
- Josef Mengele becomes chief medical officer at Auschwitz.

JUNE

- A civilian flight from Lisbon to London is shot down by Germans, killing all on board, including actor Leslie Howard.
- Military coup in Argentina ousts Ramón Castillo.
- Anti-black race riots in Detroit kills thirty-four people.

auxiliary services, the war was a time for gaining confidence in their abilities to do a man's job, and to experience an ever-widening world of opportunities discovered amidst the comradeship of other women. However, it should not be forgotten that for many other women, connected to the services by marriage as opposed to vocation, the war was a much less happy experience. Apart from the distress of having to wave their husbands goodbye when their call-up papers came through, the wives of servicemen who were not officers were often left in a very difficult financial situation.

If they had small children, they could not work themselves and therefore had to try to make-do on the low allowance the Government allotted to the wives and dependants of servicemen. An army private's wife was paid seventeen shillings a week for herself, five shillings for her first child, three shillings for the second, two for the third, and just one shilling each for every child after that. Her husband contributed seven shillings out of his own wages, leaving him with a just a bit more than a shilling a day – in sharp contrast, the allowance given to the carers of each evacuated child in Britain was eight shillings and sixpence. The pension paid to the widows of servicemen who did not return home was also small.

▲ *ID CHECK*
A little girl examines her companion's identity tag as they and other children get ready to be evacuated from London to the safety of the countryside during World War II.

ORDINARY LIFE IN EXTRAORDINARY TIMES

The country might be at war again, but the concerns of ordinary life were still uppermost in the minds of most women in Britain in September 1939. For married women, keeping a comfortable home and food on the table for their families was a major concern, as, of course, it had been since the dawn of history. As for young, unmarried women in Britain, their main object was also an age-old one: securing a partner in life with whom they could establish a home and family of their own.

Marriage in wartime became, for many, something done hastily because call-up papers had arrived in the post, or an all-too-short leave was about to expire. As for that lifetime partnership – that was something to hope for rather than to expect as a matter of right. Despite this, the marriage statistics for the six years of the war showed that the rising number of marriages in the late 1930s, perhaps reflecting increasing prosperity in the nation as a whole, was not a glitch: the boom in marriages in the first year of the war produced a record statistic of 22.5 marriages per thousand of the population. Although rates fell during the war, it has been calculated that overall, people continued to marry at the same increasing rate as they had done in the 1930s. In Britain about half a million couples married every year of the war. Women also tended to marry younger than they had in the 1930s; nearly three out of every ten brides in wartime Britain were less than twenty-one years old.

The birth-rate also soared, contrary to all expectation, given the gloom and worries about the future resulting from the war. In 1942, a year of terrible austerity, the birth-rate reached 15.6 per thousand, a rate which had not been experienced since 1931. The birth-rate continued to rise throughout the war, to reach a new peak – not surprisingly, given that thousands of servicemen were now back home after years away – of 20.6 per thousand in 1947.

A side-effect of the failure to predict the wartime rise in the birth-rate was that many items essential to the safe care of babies, including prams, teats for bottles, baby baths and fireguards, were soon either in very short supply or not available at all. As the babies became toddlers then children, their mothers found that there were very few toys for them, the government having banned the production of toys that included a long list of materials, such as rubber, cork, kapok, celluloid and plastics, that were ideal for use in children's toys. As for children's birthday

▲ *A WARTIME WEDDING*
Wartime weddings were usually done in haste, often because call-up papers had arrived in the post,
or an all-too-short leave was about to come to an end.

LATEST PRICES

ITS CLEAR
Nicholson's
Gin
ITS GOOD

Evening Standard

LATE NIGHT FINAL

La Coquille

No. 35,880   LONDON, FRIDAY, SEPTEMBER 1, 1939   ONE PENNY

GI BRIDES

When American servicemen began arriving in Britain in increasingly large numbers from mid-1942, embittered British men, especially Tommies, were soon muttering that GIs were 'overpaid, oversexed and over here'. The Tommies were right about the 'overpaid' bit: GIs had nearly seven times the pay of British servicemen, as well as seemingly unlimited supplies of chocolates, nylon stockings and other things sure to attract British girls. GIs were relaxed, generous and eager to give British girls a good time at army camp dances and in dance halls where American bands played music to jive, boogie-woogie and jitterbug to. It is not surprising that, with so many British men away overseas, thousands of British girls should have relationships with GIs. While many of these resulted in illegitimate babies who grew up never to know their fathers, nearly eighty thousand British women married American servicemen. Thousands of GI brides went to the United States after VE Day, many of them gathering with their children at reception camps, prior to boarding ships for the journey to their new lives.

parties, they would have to have streamers, paper chains and paper hats made out of newspaper because there were none of the traditional party papers made during the war, nor could there be bunches of balloons tied to the front gate or crackers to pull at the party table, on which there would probably not be an iced cake: materials and ingredients for all these were banned or simply not available.

Creating one's first home in wartime was not easy and many newly-married couples had to live with their parents or in-laws at first. Even if they did find a home of their own, they probably had little time to enjoy life in it together, with the young husband soon disappearing into the armed forces and the young wife left to look after the house while carrying on with a job and probably undertaking civil defence activities as well. Thousands of wives and mothers were left to look after the home on their own, to rescue what they could if it was bombed and could not be patched up and to find somewhere else to store their belongings while they searched for a new home. It would not have been easy for them: by the end of 1942 a million or more people were living in houses that would have been condemned in peace-time and another two and a half million families lived in bomb-damaged houses that had been given just very basic first aid.

The coming of war in 1939 put an end to the 1930s house-building boom, and in 1940 the building of new homes came to a complete halt, partly because there were not enough trained builders to construct them, but also because there were no building materials, especially timber. It was not until it became necessary to build camps and accommodation for the hundreds of thousands of

1943

JULY
- The Battle of Kursk begins.
- British paratroopers and American airborne troops commence an invasion on Sicily.
- Mussolini is overthrown in Italy.
- Operation Gomorrah – British bomb a 6 sq km area of downtown Hamburg killing 40,000 civilians in just two hours and destroying 280,000 buildings.
- Rome is bombed by the Allies for the first time in the war.

AUGUST
- John F. Kennedy's PT-boat 109 sinks at Solomon islands with the future US president on board.
- A general strike against Nazi occupation takes place in Denmark.
- Denmark scuttles the majority of its navy and Germany dissolves the Danish government.

SEPTEMBER
- Mainland Italy is invaded by Allied forces.
- New Italian government surrenders to the USA and Britain.
- Germany invades Italy, enters Rome and frees Mussolini who sets up a republic in northern Italy.
- Nazis start their liquidation of the ghettos in Minsk and Lida.
- US General Eisenhower and Italian Marshal Pietro Badoglio sign an armistice on board the British ship *Nelson*, positioned off the shore of Malta.

OCTOBER
- Naples falls to Allied soldiers.
- The new government of Italy declares war on Germany.
- Japan executes 100 US prisoners on Wake Island.

▲ *A MOVE TO THE FACTORIES*
A woman factory worker making klaxon sirens.

American servicemen who began to pour into Britain from mid-1942, that building again became a reserved occupation. In 1943 the War Cabinet at last gave the go-ahead to begin repairs on the estimated one hundred thousand houses that had been made uninhabitable by enemy action in Britain's cities and to build three thousand new cottages for agricultural workers, including for Land Girls, many of whom had moved from cities and towns to work for the Women's Land Army in the country.

Then there were the hundreds of thousands of men and women workers who moved from the danger zones to new offices, factories and armament manufacturers in the 'reception areas'. They all had to be accommodated somewhere. Hostels were built or requisitioned, but this still did not meet the demand, and so the burden fell on the householder, especially the housewife, many of whom had already had to take in evacuated children and their mothers. Many ordinary housewives, living peacefully in their homes in what had been before the war quiet market towns far from the noise and bustle of the great cities, suddenly found themselves being required to provide billets in their own homes for these workers.

Furnishing houses – even providing extra beds for billeted workers – soon became as difficult as everything else in wartime. The

▲ *FURNITURE FACTORY*
Women making utility furniture which will only be available by permit.

1943 continued . . .

OCTOBER
- British RAF conduct a second firestorm raid in Germany killing 10,000 people and rendering over 150,000 homeless.

NOVEMBER
- Lebanon gains independence from France.
- US President Franklin Roosevelt, British Prime Minister Winston Churchill and Soviet Leader Joseph Stalin meet in Tehran to discuss war strategy.

DECEMBER
- Great Depression ends in the United States.
- US President Roosevelt repels the US Chinese Exclusions Acts of 1882 and 1902. This allows Chinese residents of the US to be eligible for citizenship.
- German warship *Scharnhorst* sinks off the coast of Norway after being attacked by the British Royal Navy.
- US General Eisenhower becomes the supreme Allied commander.

Soldiers of the Reich! This day you are to take part in an offensive of such importance that the whole future of the war may depend on its outcome.

ADOLF HITLER – 5 July 1943.

demand for furniture to furnish newly-weds' homes, to replace that destroyed by enemy action and to replace what was simply worn out, could not be met by furniture makers: neither the workers nor the materials were available to meet the demand. The 'Standard Emergency Furniture' of February 1941, which was plain and simple and made of plywood, was intended as an emergency stop-gap only. Later that year, the government decided that only women and men over the age of forty could be spared to work in the furniture industry. Many women, who rather liked the relatively light and not very dangerous work in furniture factories, stayed on in the industry after the war.

The furniture situation was made worse in November 1942 when the government cut the already very small timber quota for domestic furniture by a third. The government responded in the same way as it had with the provision of food: rationing, with coupons and a points system for furniture, and the introduction of a range of 'Utility' furniture.

Utility furniture grew out of the need to make the best use of available materials, providing furniture to a minimum guaranteed standard of quality that would ensure good value for money. At first, the government had tried to counter huge price increases for both new and second-hand furniture (that made after 1900; furniture older than 1900 was 'antique' rather than 'second-hand') by bringing out a Furniture (Maximum Prices) Order in May 1942.

▶ *TABLE SHELTER*
The new indoor table shelter was introduced by the Minister of Home Security, Herbert Morrison, in the House of Commons.

THE UTILITY FURNITURE RANGE

The Board of Trade decided that the young bride wishing to buy Utility furniture for her first home should be able to choose from the Utility furniture range; a double bed, wardrobe, tallboy, dressing chest, dining table, sideboard, easy chair, three dining chairs, a kitchen table and one kitchen chair. These were the items of furniture, the Board of Trade decided, that were needed to fully furnish the average working class home. It was furniture designed to last, made only in hardwoods, which in practice, meant oak or mahogany. All joints had to be morticed or pegged, and makers had to use screws rather than pins. No plastic, which was in very short supply, could be used. The maximum price of the complete set of furniture made in oak was set at £54 9s 9d – about twenty pounds less than the same range in mahogany.

This was soon followed by the announcement of a Utility scheme for furniture. Utility furniture, which was first made available in January 1943, could only be bought with coupons and was available only to three 'priority classes': newly married couples setting up home for the first time, couples needing homes because babies were on the way, or those who had been bombed out. These priority cases were issued with 'dockets', or ' buying permits', to buy furniture up to the value of a specific number of 'units', depending on the nature of their need for furniture.

When the first Utility furniture, which was the work of three leading designers, was put on show, together with Wedgwood's Victory Ware crockery and some Utility cookware, for three weeks at the Building Centre in central London in October 1942, thirty thousand people visited the exhibition. Most visitors liked it because, although basic in design, it was plain and solid, reminding many of the furniture of the Arts and Crafts movement. Reaction was similar in Glasgow and other cities where the furniture was exhibited. The Utility furniture scheme was later extended to include curtain materials, bedlinen and mattresses and the floor covering, linoleum.

As in so many other aspects of life in Britain, World War II dramatically changed attitudes to sex out of wedlock, to marriage itself and to divorce and the birth of children. It wasn't just that women, while remaining the nation's home-makers, discovered that they could also make a major contribution to the world that went on outside the home. They also discovered that it was possible to hold down a worthwhile job while still maintaining a happy home life.

Before the war, women, despite their hard-won experience and training as secretaries, teachers and nurses, had automatically lost their jobs when they married. It was recognised well before the war that this situation would have to change, if only 'for the duration'. Thousands of women were recalled from marriage or retirement to take up their old jobs in teaching, nursing and other professions. By the end of September 1939, the Ministry of Health's Emergency Medical Service had already enrolled fifteen thousand trained nurses and twenty thousand trained auxiliaries.

Although most married women were forced unwillingly to return to their place in the home at the end of the war, post-war society put very different demands on men and women alike than the society of the 1930s had; within a couple of decades of the end of the war, women were going back out to work in numbers that soon exceeded wartime figures.

For many women, having become used to being solely in charge of the home while their husbands served in the armed forces, the end of the war and the return of their menfolk took some getting used to. The majority of women were pleased and relieved to have their husbands and the fathers of their children home; a quite sizeable minority were not. Divorce rates in Britain soared during and after the war.

▶ *SAVING WHAT YOU CAN*
After their home was destroyed during a German air raid, a father and son load a horse-drawn cart with the family furniture while moving from their bombed out East End home.

There were just under ten thousand divorce petitions in 1938, and twenty-five thousand in 1945.

True, many of the post-war divorces were between young couples who had married in haste, when one of them was due to be called up, and were now repenting at leisure. But many more were between couples who found that their wartime experiences had irrevocably changed them and their attitudes towards each other. Loneliness and a lack of sexual fulfilment led many women into adulterous relationships during the war – a fact of life implicitly acknowledged in the many articles in women's magazines that talked about the importance of a woman's loyalty in thought and deed towards her husband serving in the armed forces – so it is not surprising that more than two-thirds of divorce petitions in 1945 were on the grounds of adultery.

The other rate that, not surprisingly, soared during the war was that of illegitimate births. One-third of all births in Britain during World War II were illegitimate – at a time when the overall birth rate declined at a rate faster than it had already been doing in the 1930s. It would be natural to assume that many of these illegitimate births occurred because young women could not bear to send their young lovers off to the wars with just a chaste kiss and a wave of the hand. But statistics show that illegitimate births were much higher among older women than younger ones: 'spinsters kicking over the traces as they neared middle-age', as the historian Angus Calder put it. And it should not be forgotten that many fathers were servicemen, and were simply not there to make an honest woman of their pregnant girlfriends.

A much more basic reason for the rise in illegitimacy rates was the suddenly altered lifestyles of young women. Thousands of them were released from the eagle eyes of their parents and the confines of home when they were as young as fifteen or seventeen, often into digs, billets and the shared accommodation of service barracks far from their home towns and villages. Their newly relaxed lifestyles took them after work or off duty into pubs and dance halls where they could forget the drab and austere conditions of their lives. Many girls lost their virginity during one-night stands enjoyed without a thought of the consequences the morrow was all too likely to bring.

◄ *WAITING FOR MUM*
Babies sit in line in their prams at the Muriel Green Nursery Centre, St Albans, where they are looked after whilst their mothers are working for the war effort.

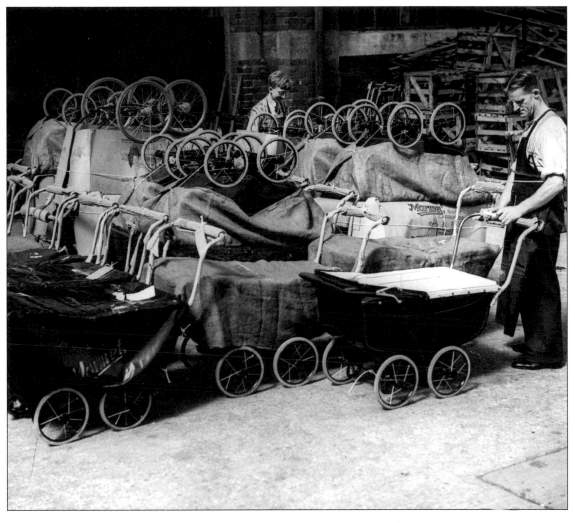

▲ *Pram Factory*
Workers at a Marmet pram factory in Letchworth, Hertfordshire, do their best to solve the shortage of baby carriages in Britain during World War II.

At the start of the war, there was nowhere unmarried women could go to get contraceptive advice and nowhere 'safe' they could go to for an abortion or for adoption advice. Society condemned them for their immorality; even in hospital maternity wards they were segregated from married pregnant women. However, unmarried mothers were accepted back into society – together with their children – more readily than in the past, partly because there were so many of them it helped to desensitise the issue. As in so many other social matters, the conditions of wartime life taught the post-war world to be less condemning of women who gave birth outside the bounds of marriage – and much more accepting of the children, too.

A HEALTHY DIET FOR ALL

The surprising thing about life in wartime Britain, which before the war relied on its merchant fleet – like its navy, the largest in the world – to bring to Britain much of its food from all parts of the world, was that nobody starved. Many people often felt hungry, but seldom desperately so. In fact, nutritionists and food experts – the well-known food writer Marguerite Patten, for instance – believe that, on the whole, Britain was very well fed during World War II, being provided with one of the most nutritionally sound diets the nation had ever known.

Government planners recognised that should war come, there would very quickly be reductions in food imports once German U-boats were at large in the North Atlantic, as this was where all merchant shipping bound for Britain, whether from North America or much further away, ended up. They thought they could plan for this, perhaps even without having to bring in rationing, which had become necessary towards the end of World War I.

Even though the U-boat menace in the Atlantic had been largely neutralised by the end of 1943, food imports remained at a seriously lower level than before 1939. When Germany overran Europe and Italy entered the war in 1940, the Mediterranean was virtually closed to merchant shipping coming through the Suez Canal, the route for food imports from Asia and Australia, and Japan's war in the Far East cut back imports of tea, rice and cane sugar (at a time when the import of cane sugar from the West Indies was also much diminished). The loss of sugar imports turned sugar beet into a widely grown crop in wartime Britain, with the beets being processed in large factories converted from other uses.

One of the government's earliest decisions, before war was declared, was to bring an additional two million acres under the plough as soon as possible. At much the same time, the old World War I Women's Land Army was reconvened to recruit women over the age of seventeen to work on the land. The effect was to bring women into the food supply business as more than just housewives and cooks.

Not that women saw themselves as 'just housewives and cooks'. Even before the government had launched its Dig for Victory campaign, women were working out how to make the best use of their back gardens, window boxes and even the roof of their Anderson shelters to grow food or raise hens, pigs and rabbits. People also began cultivating allotments – many of them in public parks and gardens – with enthusiasm.

▲   *DIG FOR VICTORY*
An assortment of posters used to launch the government's Dig for Victory campaign.

A WARTIME GARDEN IN LANCASHIRE

At the height of the Munich Crisis in 1938, Nella Last devised a plan to make the best use of her garden in Barrow-in-Furness. Within a day of war being declared in September 1939, as she wrote in the diary she kept for Mass-Observation, she had revived and polished up her plan. She would 'keep hens on half the lawn. The other half of the lawn will grow potatoes, and cabbage will grow under the apple trees and among the currant bushes. I'll try and buy this year's pullets and only get six, but when spring comes I'll get two sittings and have about twenty extra hens in the summer to kill,' wrote the indomitable 'housewife, 49', as she described herself at the start of her diary. 'I know a little about keeping hens and I'll read up.' Her husband laughed, but said 'Go ahead'.

There were some 800,000 allotments in England and Wales in 1939; by 1945 the number had risen to 1.5 million.

In 1937, the government, foreseeing that it would have to be closely involved in the management of food supplies in wartime, set up a Food Department (renamed the Ministry of Food after the outbreak of war, and given Lord Woolton as its head). One of the Ministry of Food's first big jobs was to organise the drawing up of a National Register of adults, children and infants as a prelude to issuing everyone with food ration books. Ration books, issued in September 1939, contained coupons covering the purchase of rationed foods and were coloured, according to the group the book's holder belonged to: cream books for adults, green for children and blue for babies and infants.

The government, misreading, not for the first time, the mood of the people, put off actually beginning the rationing of food because it thought the move would be unpopular. In fact, the general feeling was that rationing would give everyone a fair share of what was available, so that when the government did start rationing food, beginning in January 1940 with bacon, sugar and butter, no one complained.

Ration books were to become the bane of everyone's life, especially for the wife and

◀ *MAKING THE MOST OF AN ANDERSON SHELTER*
Women needed to find ways of making the best use of their back gardens – window boxes and even the roof of their Anderson shelters were used to grow fresh vegetables.

THE NATIONAL LOAF

Bread was not rationed during the war (although it had to be after it, largely because of poor world wheat harvests just after the war). Although something like a seventh of the nation's flour milling capacity was destroyed during the Blitz, women could still buy white bread, and the white flour for making their own, until about mid-1942. By this time, the amounts of wheat getting into the country from abroad were so low that the extraction rate for wheat had to be greatly increased so that much more of each precious grain of wheat could be used. The wartime National Wheatmeal Loaf was not popular, despite everything the Ministry of Food said about its nutritional value. It was coarse and grey and many people, including Ernest Bevin, the Minister of Labour, complained – loudly, during a meeting of the War Cabinet – that it was indigestible.

mother who did the family shopping. One could not just walk into the nearest shop, buy what one wanted and hand over the ration book for the correct coupons to be deducted. Every ration book had to have written inside it the names of the retailers the customer was registered with; counterfoils of the registration forms were kept by the shopkeeper. This was because shops were allowed only enough rationed foods to cover registered customers, plus some extras to allow for servicemen and women at home on leave.

Ration books and coupons, plus the monthly points system, allowing the purchase of 'extras', such as a can of fish or meat, or specific weights of dried fruits or pulses, gave shopkeepers headaches, too, because they had to file carefully the registration counterfoils, fill in dozens of forms for the Ministry, count all the coupons they took, and then take the forms and coupons to their local Food Office. Shopkeepers had to be fully aware of all the alterations to the rations, such as changes in quantities and prices, that the Ministry was constantly making.

Foods rationed in Britain during the war, with the permitted amounts varying from time to time, depending on availability, were: meat, except for offal, though it was occasionally rationed, and sausages, which were rarely seen in the butcher's shop; bacon and ham; butter, cheese, margarine and cooking fat; milk, including fresh milk and dried milk (chocolate and ice cream manufacturers were

◀ *WARTIME HARVEST*
Women gathering in the rye harvest in East Suffolk, since the wartime announcement that the crop may now be used in Britain's bread.

1944

JANUARY
- The *Daily Mail* becomes the first transoceanic newspaper.
- The Royal Air Force drops 2,300 bombs on Berlin.
- The Allies begin Operation Shingle – an assault on Anzio, Italy.
- Russian troops recapture Novgorod, and retake Leningrad one week later.
- US forces land on the Japanese-held Marshall Islands.

FEBRUARY
- US troops capture the Marshall Islands.
- The Battle of Eniwetok Atoll begins on the Marshall Islands. The battle ended in a US victory.
- The Admiralty Islands are invaded by troops led by US General Douglas MacArthur.

MARCH
- The leader of the 1930s crime syndicate Murder Inc, Louis Buchalter, is exected at Sing Sing.
- Nazi forces occupy Hungary.
- 335 Italians (many of whom were civilians) were shot by German troops in the Fosse Ardeantine caves outside Rome.

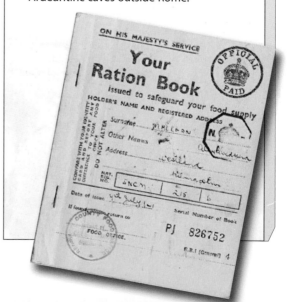

▲ *THE RURAL PIE SCHEME*
Pies were distributed daily to make sure that agricultural workers got a nutritious lunch every day.

THE RURAL PIE SCHEME

A splendid WVS initiative, begun at harvest time in Cambridgeshire in 1941, when they supplied a daily hot pie service to the workers in the fields, led to the Rural Pie Scheme. The Ministry of Food, seeing how the WVS women had managed to cook and distribute some seventy thousand pies, was soon advising local authorities on how they could launch similar schemes, using commercial catering firms, to ensure that agricultural workers got a nutritious lunch every day. At its peak, the Rural Pie Scheme was carrying pies and other snacks to agricultural workers in the fields around some five thousand villages at an average rate of one and a quarter million snacks a week.

prohibited from using milk in their products); sugar, with extra sometimes being made available at jam-making time; preserves; tea; eggs; and sweets.

Queuing, often for hours, outside shops in all weathers became a way of life for women during the war. With just one or two shop assistants behind the counter to find, weigh and wrap every woman's purchases, and to take the correct number of coupons from the family's ration books, shopping became a very long process.

The Ministry of Food did its best to help relieve the boredom and austerity of wartime food, at the same time waging constant war against waste: 'Food is a munition of war. Don't Waste It' said the Ministry's posters. The Ministry produced a long series of 'Food Facts' booklets, leaflets and pamphlets intended to keep housewives well informed about what foods were available, what their nutritional values were, and how they could be best prepared and used in cooking. The last-mentioned was very needed, especially when unfamiliar items like dried egg powder and skimmed milk powder (called household milk) first appeared, to be followed later in the war by even more unlikely things like snook and whalemeat.

Throughout the war, from July 1940, the BBC Home Service broadcast a five-minute programme about food and cooking called 'Kitchen Front' at 8.15 a.m. from Tuesday to Friday. It was timed so that it would catch housewives after breakfast and before they went out to do their day's shopping. Since it was part of the Kitchen Front's task to alert women to what foods were currently available, the programme's contributors often had the difficult task of thinking up exciting and interesting ways of preparing carrots, potatoes and oatmeal – all too often the only foods widely available.

From the outset, the government was particularly concerned about the health of mothers and babies. Free or cheap milk was always made available for them. The children's Vitamin Welfare Scheme, launched at the end of 1941, provided free blackcurrant juice and cod liver oil for children under two, with the blackcurrant juice being replaced by orange juice when the Lend-lease scheme began bringing orange juice from America. If a shipment of fresh oranges made it past U-boat attack and into the country, greengrocers were expected to keep them solely for children for the first five days they were in the shops.

Feeding people after air raids, both in the immediate aftermath, and for weeks and months afterwards while power lines and gas supplies were restored and houses rebuilt, was a major headache for the government. It was one that women played a big part in relieving, especially the women of the WVS, bringing their mobile canteens and Queen's Messengers convoys to the sites of air raids. The WVS were also good at demonstrating how to build efficient temporary ovens in the street, using bricks and rubble from damaged buildings. Then there were the housewives themselves, increasingly adept at building their own temporary cooking facilities in the garden or the street, and, of course, sharing their own undamaged kitchens with less fortunate neighbours.

When the Food Leaders scheme, a development of the Food Convoys and the Food Flying Squads that replaced them, was launched nationally in 1944, most of the fifteen thousand Leaders appointed before the end of the war in 1945 were WVS housewives. Their job was basically a public education task: to advise people how to make the best of what foods were available so that everyone would have a diet that was nutritious enough, even if not always very delicious or interesting, to keep them in good health.

By far the most attractive government initiative to feed the people in wartime Britain – apart from the school meals scheme which by 1945 was giving one in three schoolchildren a daily meal, and the boom in providing good canteens in factories – was the British Restaurants scheme. British Restaurants were a development of the post-air raid welfare centres and Communal Feeding Centres, especially the Londoners' Meal Service of the Blitz, that the government developed to deal with the aftermath of bombing raids. Women provided most of the staff at Communal Feeding Centres, having first undertaken a course in feeding large numbers nutritiously and cheaply at training schools. They were also the staff at British Restaurants, which provided cheap and healthy meals, usually based on unrationed foods, to thousands of men and women every day.

British Restaurants – their name was a piece of inspired thinking by the Prime Minister, Winston Churchill – were provided by local authorities, and were operated on a non-profit-making basis. Because of the latter provision, they were vehemently opposed by private restaurant and café owners, and some local authorities did not show much enthusiasm for opening them. Where the government had hoped for 10,000

▲ *TEMPORARY OVENS*
Housewives became adept at making their own temporary cooking facilities in the garden or the street. Here a passer-by examines the ingenuity of this dustbin oven built into a brick wall.

HUNGER IN THE CHANNEL ISLANDS

The people of Britain came through the war reasonably well fed and in reasonable health. The same could not be said for the majority of Channel Islanders. Within months of the German invasion in July 1940, the people of the Channel Islands were facing severe food shortages and by the time they were liberated in May 1945, many were close to starvation. Between the two dates were years of families hiding what food there was from the German occupying forces and of housewives cooking their food and baking their bread (made from a mixture of corn, water and salt, and called 'hard bake') in communal ovens because there was no fuel for home ovens. Eventually, many were eating either potatoes, including the peelings, or cabbage soup day after day – and eating any slugs found among the cabbage leaves because of their precious protein content. Tea was made from brambles and jelly from seaweed.

Two women from the Channel Islands make the most of what they have and make a nutritious dandelion salad.

British Restaurants, only some 2,160 had opened by the autumn of 1943. At their peak, British Restaurants were serving more than 600,000 meals a day, on a self-service basis to save on staff. The food was good, and the atmosphere pleasant and friendly.

British Restaurants and the nation's many privately run restaurants, in which the Ministry of Food capped the price of a meal at 5 shillings (25p) early in the war, provided oases of good company in a difficult world and contributed greatly to the development of the 'eating out' habit that was a mark of social life in wartime Britain – and which continued on into peacetime.

▲ *CARROTS ON STICKS*
Three young children enjoy a portable, healthy snack – a carrot on a stick. Ice cream is not available due to war rationing, so anything like this is a real treat.

LOOKING GOOD ON LESS

When the women's pages of Britain's national newspapers and women's magazines published articles emphasising the importance of women making the best of themselves in wartime, and not just because it was important to look their best when their husbands came home, they were simply following government guidelines. Keeping up the nation's morale was seen by the government as essential to winning the war.

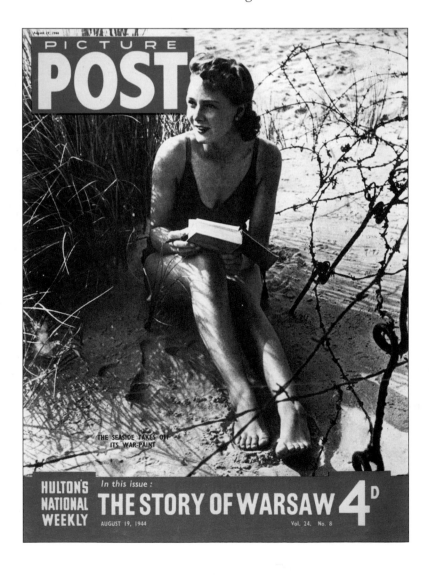

Women's magazines accepted the morale-boosting part they were expected to play from the outset. As *Vogue* put it in their September 1939 issue: 'We can't speak for the future in these times, but on the date this goes to press, *Vogue* is still at the old addresses... We started our A.R.P. arrangements in August 1938, and had them all ready last March. So with the consent – indeed, at the desire – of our staff, we remain on the job, in the places where our various departments can best serve their customers.' In other words, whatever their jobs, whatever their class in society, Britain's women were all going to 'see it through' together.

Fabrics and textiles for home dress-making, which had enjoyed a boom among women in the 1920s and 1930s with the availability of inexpensive, easy-to-use sewing machines, quickly became hard to find from early in the war, as did wool for knitting. First came restrictions, imposed by the Board of Trade, on the use of many textiles, including silk and artificial silk, rayon, leather, wool, cotton and flax (for linen). Silk was needed for parachutes, and wool for uniforms. Despite this, clothes rationing was not brought in until June, 1941. At first there were no dedicated clothing ration books, and people were

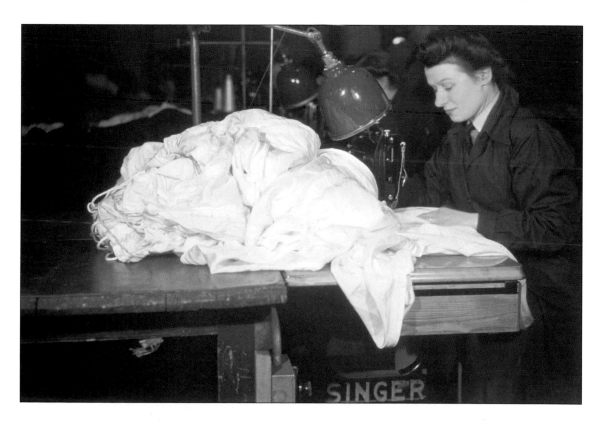

◄ *AND THE WAR RAGES ON*
The cover of Picture Post *in August 1944, shows a young woman relaxing on a British beach with a book, but a tangle of barbed wire reminds her that the war is still raging in Europe.*

▲ *A USE FOR SILK*
A WAAF woman uses a Singer sewing machine to stitch a bundle of parachute silk.

NUMBER OF COUPONS REQUIRED

WOMEN AND GIRLS

	Adult	Child
Lined mackintosh or coat	14	11
Jacket, or short coat	11	8
Dress or frock – woollen	11	8
Dress or frock – other material	7	5
Gym tunic	8	6
Blouse, sports shirt, cardigan or jumper	5	3
Skirt	7	5
Overalls or dungarees	6	4
Apron or pinafore	3	2
Pyjamas	8	6
Nightdress	6	5
Petticoat or slip, combination or cami-knickers	4	3
Other undergarments, including corsets	3	2
Pair of stockings	2	1
Pair of socks (ankle length)	1	1
Collar, tie or pair of cuffs	1	1
Two handkerchiefs	1	1
Scarf, pair of gloves, mittens or muff	2	2
Pair of slippers, boots or shoes	5	3

instructed to use twenty-six 'spare' margarine coupons from their food ration books instead. The first clothing ration books were issued in mid-1942.

It is possible that the Prime Minister himself had something to do with this quite late date for clothes rationing. As Oliver Lyttelton, President of the Board of Trade in 1940-41, recalled in the ITV television series, *The World at War*, Churchill was opposed to anything that might dampen civilian morale and thus affect output and lengthen the time needed to win the war. But, to Oliver Lyttelton the reason for bringing in clothes rationing was a simple matter of manpower, with the difference between rationed clothes and free clothes being four hundred and fifty thousand workers. As for the morale thing, Oliver Lyttelton told Churchill that he thought 'the population wanted to do something, particularly the women, after Dunkirk, to feel they were part of the war.'

Oliver Lyttelton turned out to have a more sensitive finger on the national pulse than the Prime Minister did. There was little complaining about and a general acceptance of clothes rationing, with people 'glad to be a little bit shabby and [feeling] that they were doing their stint', as Lyttelton put it.

People might have been less accepting of the need to be a bit shabby if they had known that clothing rationing would not end in Britain until 1949. Anyway, as many people discovered very quickly, there was always the black market, which thrived in the early days of clothes rationing because people could claim that their coupon books had been lost or stolen and have them replaced by handfuls of loose coupons. In 1943, when the Board of Trade estimated that some 700,000 clothing coupon books

USING CLOTHING COUPONS

In the first fifteen months of clothing rationing, everyone was allocated 66 coupons. For the fourteen months from July 1942 to September 1943, they were allocated only 40, with a rise to 48 in the following year. The allocation for the year after September 1945, when women should have been celebrating victory with a bright new wardrobe, dropped to just 36 coupons, largely because there was a serious shortage of textile mill workers. Here are examples of what a woman could use her coupons to purchase: a suit needed 18 coupons, plus the purchase price, which soared as the war went on; a lined winter coat, 18 coupons (an unlined coat was 15 coupons, reflecting the smaller amount of material needed to make it); a blouse, 5 coupons; a cotton or rayon dress, 7 coupons; a winter woollen dress, 11 coupons; a pair of stockings (increasingly hard to obtain, anyway), 2 coupons. Women's hats were not subject to clothes rationing; even so military-style berets, or fabric turbans, as worn by all women, from workers in factories to Clementine Churchill, the Prime Minister's wife, became more popular than hats.

had been 'lost' or 'stolen', the system was changed so that loose coupons were no longer acceptable. Coupons in the new books issued that year were not taken out when clothing was bought, but instead were stamped to indicate that they had been used to buy clothing.

At the same time as clothes rationing was introduced, the government's propaganda machine swung into action under the banner of another of its famous wartime slogans: 'Make Do and

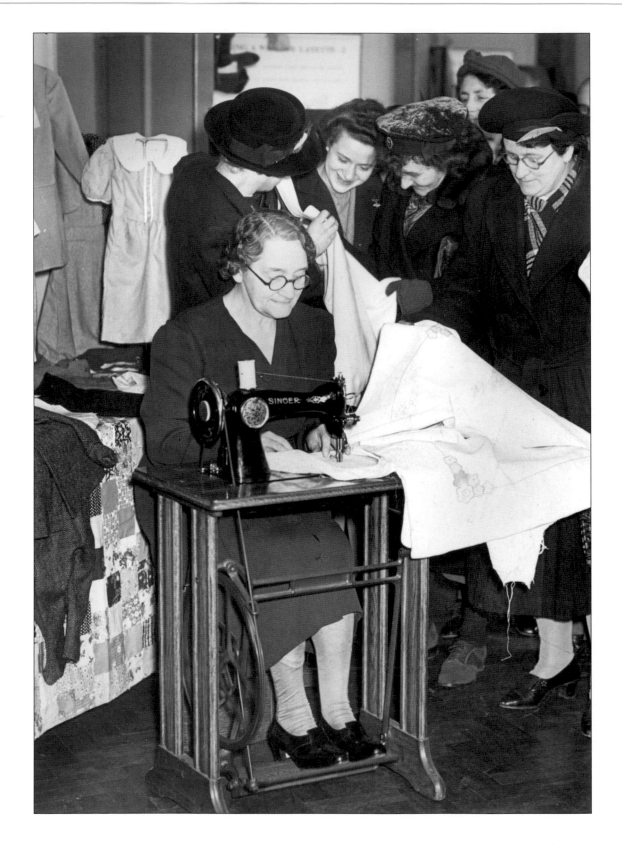

Mend'. Much of the make do and mend campaign now seems both patronising towards women and very 'nanny state'. Women did not need Her Majesty's Stationery Office to issue posters, emanating from the Board of Trade, advising them to 'Go through your wardrobe' and sort out clothes for mending or refurbishing, or to 'Make Do and Mend' by sewing 'decorative' patches over worn parts, keeping clothes packed away from moths, and unpicking and re-knitting sweaters. Women could work out such things for themselves.

It is possible that without the advice included in a Board of Trade booklet, few women would have thought to make themselves skirts out of their husband's old plus-fours or turn his waistcoat into a top for themselves by adding sleeves knitted from odd balls of wool. But perhaps they would have, for women showed great ingenuity in making themselves clothes out of the unlikeliest material during the war. With *Gone With the Wind* among the most popular films shown in wartime Britain, it is not surprising that women emulated Scarlett

◀ *A STITCH IN TIME*
A wartime clothing factory worker demonstrates how to renovate old clothes.

▲ *CHEAP LABOUR*
Even children turned their hand to knitting during the war.

1944

APRIL
- A huge explosion occurs at the Bombay harbour killing 300 people.
- Women in France get the right to vote.
- Americans launch Operation Persecution in the Pacific. Allied forces land in the Hollandia area of New Guinea.

MAY
- Mahatma Gandhi is freed from prison.
- The Allies start a major offensive against the Axis Powers on the Gustav Line.
- The type IX U-boat is launched.
- SS troops burn down six villages in the Brkini hills in south west Slovenia.

JUNE
- The Allies enter Rome.
- The Allies land in Normandy and begin the invasion of France – D-Day.
- Germany commences bombing of Britain with V1 bombs.
- More than 600 people are massacred by German troops in the French town of Oradour-sur-Glane.
- Iceland becomes independent from Denmark and forms a republic.
- Battle of the Philippine Sea where the US Navy sank three Japanese aircraft carriers and shot down almost 400 aircraft in what they called 'The Marianas Turkey Shoot'.

JULY
- The Russian city of Minsk is retaken by Russian troops and 100,000 Germans are captured.
- Hundreds of Japanese civilians commit suicide under the threat of US occupation of Saipan.
- An assassination attempt on Hitler, planned by some of his own generals, is unsuccessful.
- General Kuniaka Koiso becomes prime minister of Japan.

O'Hara – who tore down the velvet curtains in the drawing room to make herself a dress grand enough to disguise her real poverty – and made dresses, blouses and skirts out of curtains that had had to be taken down and replaced by blackout materials. More surprising, perhaps, is the use of old sugar bags and sacking, chamois leather (bought before the war to clean windows), hessian and canvas to make clothes. Later in the war, parachute nylon and silk were also much sought after, with the latter making fine petticoats, camisoles and other feminine underwear.

With so many women looking smart in the uniforms of the auxiliary services and the various Civil Defence units, many others doing men's work in dungarees and trousers, and even volunteers wearing uniforms – the WVS's winter great coat was designed by the London fashion house of Digby Morton – it is not surprising that women's fashions took on a distinctly military style during the war. The two-piece suit, with its short, square, shoulder-padded jacket and knee-length straight skirt is ubiquitous in photographs of this period. Women wore their suits to work, when they went out in the evenings and even for their wedding: after all, the young man whose arm every bride held was almost invariably wearing a service uniform.

The Board of Trade's increasingly draconian rulings on the style, shape and fabric content of the nation's clothing reached a climax in 1943 with the production of the first range of Utility clothing. The Board chose the distinctly uninspiring name 'utility' in 1941 to apply to a new range of good-quality products (in terms of design and materials) that could be sold at reasonable prices. The first such product,

▲ *A SAFE PLACE FOR MONEY*
This was a corset designed with pockets for members of the ATS and WAAF at their own request. Their uniform only has pockets in the jackets so when these are removed for work as they often are there is no safe place for their money hence this corset design.

which preceded Utility furniture by a few months, was Utility clothing, announced in the Civilian Clothing Order of June 1942. Eventually Utility clothing came to account for almost eighty per cent of all clothing production.

The first thirty-two items of women's and men's Utility clothing were unveiled to the public at a special display in September 1942. The clothes, which included women's dresses, suits and coats, shirts and top coats for men, had been designed by eight of London's leading fashion designers, including Norman Hartnell, Hardy Amies and Digby Morton. They were shown in the first fashion show to feature both female and male mannequins. The clothes were surprisingly attractive, belying that dreary-sounding 'utililty' label. Even *Vogue* approved of both the styles, which 'pared away superfluities', and fabrics used, reporting that 'all women now have equal chance to buy beautifully designed clothes suitable to their lives and incomes'. In a burst of patriotic enthusiasm, *Vogue* called the Utility clothing scheme 'an outstanding example of applied democracy.'

▶ *WARTIME FASHION*
Despite the austerity that wartime inevitably imposed, women discovered that fashion need not necessarily be a drab affair.

THE UTILITY MARK'S CHEESES

When the first Utility clothes went on sale in spring 1943 they all bore a label showing the Utility trademark logo which was to become very familiar to the buyers of clothes, bed linen and furniture during the war and for some time afterwards. The label carried the Utility scheme symbol, consisting of two heavy, round black spots with a wedge cut out of one edge of each to give 'C' shapes; it was not long before Board of Trade staff were referring to Reginald Shipp's original and modern design as 'the two cheeses'. The number '41' worked into the wedge of the second 'C' completed the logo, 'CC41', short for 'Civilian Clothing 1941'. Women came to look out for the Utility Mark in clothes because it indicated that they had been made with good quality fabric and that the price had been rigorously controlled.

There were two main objectives behind the Board of Trade's 'Austerity Regulations' that restricted the styles of Utility clothes to just a few shapes, and forbade the use of more than three buttons on a women's suit or the use of complicated trimmings such as embroidery or appliqué work. One was to limit the use of very scarce raw materials; the other was to encourage long and therefore economical production runs. Even underwear was subject to stringent regulations. Underneath their smart Utility suits and dresses, women could wear underwear chosen from a range of just six shapes. No wonder women queued to buy used parachutes and unwanted parachute silk: it made delightful underwear.

Children, like their parents, were issued with clothes ration books, so it is not surprising that knitting and sewing clothes for their children became just another important task that women had to find time for during the war. Once again, the WVS came to the rescue, setting up clothing exchanges where mothers could take the clothes their children had outgrown in the hope that they could exchange them for others that would fit them.

Just as important to a woman's morale as clothing, and the ability to replace it when it wore out, was make-up. During the 1930s make-up, no longer the preserve of young and 'fast' women, began to be worn by women of all ages. There had been many advances in make-up production in the inter-

◀ *OLD SILK STOCKINGS*
Old silk stockings were collected by the WVS because airmen used to use them under their own socks as an additional means of keeping warm. They were also a good way of keeping bandages clean.

1944

AUGUST
- The Frank family are captured by the Gestapo after being in hiding for more than two years.
- Paris is liberated by Allied troops after four years of German occupation.
- The Soviet Union invades Romania.
- Romania switches sides and attacks Hungary.

SEPTEMBER
- Belgium is liberated by the Allies.
- Soviet Union declare war on Bulgaria.
- Germany begins bombing of Britain with V2 rockets.
- Allied troops invade Germany.
- Soviet Union invade Czechoslovakia.
- Roosevelt and Churchill meet in Quebec as part of the Octagon Conference to discuss war strategy.
- Troops from Canada, Great Britain and the USA parachute into Arnhem, Netherlands, as part of Operation Market Garden.
- Armistice between Finland and Soviet Union ends the Continuation War.
- Germans defeat British at Arnhem.

OCTOBER
- Soviet Union invade Yugoslavia.
- Rommel commits suicide after a failed coup against Hitler.
- Largest naval battle in history begins in Leyte Gulf, the Red Army enters Hungary.
- The Japanese aircraft carrier *Zuikaku* is sunk.
- Allied forces invade the Philippines.
- The Soviet Union invades Germany.

NOVEMBER
- Allies liberate Greece.
- Roosevelt is elected for a fourth term.
- Nazi troops invade Albania.
- The first human surgery to correct blue baby syndrome is performed by Alfred Blalock and Vivien Thomas.

war years, including such things as lipsticks in a wide range of bright colours, such as Schiaparelli's famous Shocking pink, new types of mascara and eyeshadow, special massage creams and make-up with a built-in sun protection factor.

A Limitations of Supply Order, passed early in the war, stopped or cut to a bare minimum production of much of this kind of make-up, since its materials were needed for other things. So the women of the war years 'made do' with the material to hand. Boot polish made an acceptable mascara, rose petals steeped for weeks in wine provided a substitute for rouge and beetroot juice was used to colour the lips. Since lipstick was still produced by hand, even the most advanced machines turning out only 144 lipsticks at a time, its production was limited during the war, with much that was sold coming in wooden cases, to preserve precious metal supplies. If a woman was lucky, she might be able to get hold of one of the anti-sunburn lipsticks produced for the troops in 1943.

Britain's young women, nothing if not enterprising, even found a make-up to replace silk stockings. Early on, young women contrived to make their own leg paints at home from such simple things as gravy browning. But soon cosmetics manufacturers were getting in on the act and producing leg paints with names that suggested they were 'liquid silk stockings'. Painted on the legs, these products made an acceptable substitute for no longer available silk stockings. The addition of a line carefully drawn down the back of the leg with an eyebrow pencil or a soft drawing pencil completed the effect.

Even after American GIs began arriving in Britain in force, bringing silk stockings and nylons with them, women who wanted the effect of stockings on bare legs continued to paint their own legs, or else went to a leg colouring bar in their local department store or beauty salon. Paying threepence (just over 1p) for each leg painted in the shade of their choice was a small price for a women to pay for good-looking legs.

Perhaps the most difficult aspect of wartime women's beauty was the maintenance of a head of shining, well-cut and well-maintained hair. A shortage of metal hair pins, hair cosmetics, shampoos and perming solutions accounted for the greatly increased use of hairnets and the popularity

of the head-covering turban. Despite such problems, fashionable women's hairstyles, based on longer hair, became increasingly complicated, with hair being rolled into many different styles. The styles were even given patriotic names, such as the 'Victory V' (as shown above by the actress Rita Hayworth) the 'Montgomery's Sweet' or even the 'Ack Ack', by enterprising hairdressers.

▶ *A STEADY HAND*
A Max Factor beautician paints a seam on a woman's leg to help create the illusion of stockings during a World War II shortage.

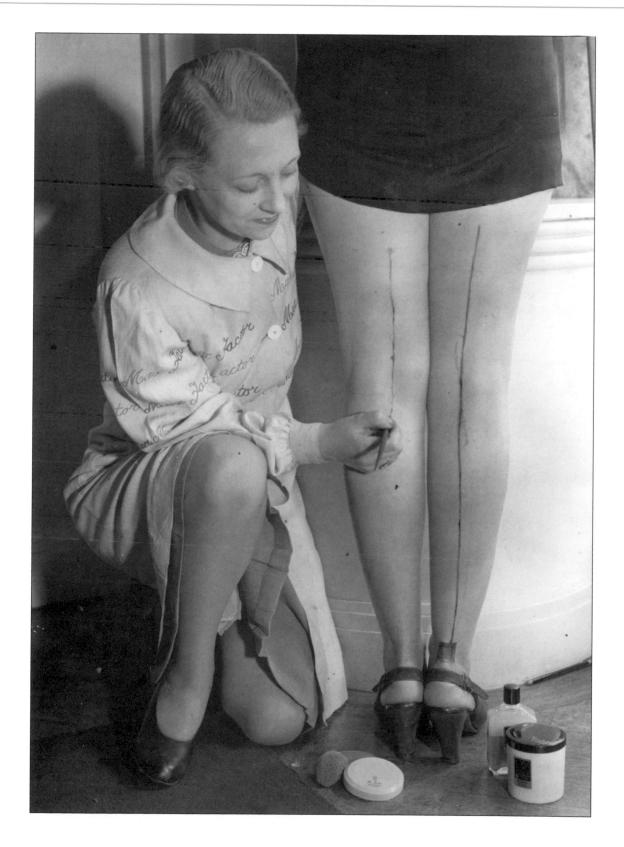

PEACE AND THE SLOW RETURN TO NORMALITY

Women greeted peace in 1945 with a reaction that mixed relief and a certain cynicism. What was there to celebrate in a country heavily damaged by war and marked by austerity and exhaustion? As Nella Last noted in her diary, even the announcement by Stuart Hibbard on the BBC's Home Service that 8 May 1945 would be celebrated as Victory in Europe Day came as something of a damp squib – 'What a FLOP!'. And what were the rosettes and tri-coloured buttonholes in the shop windows all about? But, 'we must celebrate somehow,' thought Mrs Last, so she went into her kitchen, put the kettle on, and looked into the cupboard.
'I'll open this tin of pears.' And she did.

Nella Last was right to be careful about the contents of her kitchen cupboard, even when celebrating victory. Food rationing was to last in Britain for another nine years. For a time, it even became more severe, partly because of a worldwide shortage of basic foods and grains, and partly because the winter of 1946–7 was exceptionally severe and led to poor harvests. The ending of the American Lend-Lease programme after VJ Day in August 1945, by which time there had been a General Election which had swept the Labour Party, led by Clement Atlee, into power, meant that there were no more shipments of such useful foods as dried eggs and dried milk coming into Britain.

◀ *WINSTON CHURCHILL*
Prime Minister of Great Britain Winston Churchill (1874–1965) makes his VE Day Broadcast to the world.

▲ *WORLDWIDE SHORTAGE*
Even after the war there was a worldwide shortage of basic foods and grains. For that reason rationing was to last for another nine years.

POST-WAR RATIONING

Goods	Allowance
Bacon and ham	2 oz per person a fortnight
Cheese	1½ oz a week
Butter/margarine	7 oz a week
Cooking fats	2 oz a week
Meat	1s worth a week
Sugar	8 oz a week
Tea	2 oz a week
Chocolates and sweets	4 oz a week
Eggs	No fixed ration. 1 egg for each ration book when available
Liquid milk	3 pints a week
Preserves	4 oz a week
Points-rationed food per week	4 points

Also rationed:
Bread
Soap
Bananas
Potatoes

REGISTER HERE
FOR ALL
RATIONED
FOODS
GOOD STOCKS
AND
Fair Distribution
of Unrationed Articles
ASK
SATISFIED CUSTOMERS

The government could not be blamed for bringing Lend-Lease to an end as quickly as possible, as the scheme had to be paid for and was expensive, but its ending did add in the short term to the country's food problems. One way of helping relieve the problems was to keep the Women's Land Army hard at work for another five years. The WLA stood down at the end of 1950, their last duty being a ceremonial parade at Buckingham Palace, where they were reviewed by Queen Elizabeth. The Queen let it be known that she felt the parade had been a fitting climax to the notable history of the Women's Land Army. The government did not make any special pension available for Land Girls, however.

Early in 1946 the amounts of the butter, margarine and fat rations had to be reduced. And in the summer, bread, which had remained unrationed (even if of poor quality) throughout the war had to be rationed in July, and was not de-rationed again until 1948. In November 1947, it was the turn of potatoes, which also had not been rationed before, to be added to the still long list of foods for which the housewife had to find ration coupons. A year later, the food situation took a turn for the better, when the President of the Board of Trade, the future prime minister Harold Wilson, made a root and branch attack on the food controls that had built up since 1940.

▶ *PLEASE SIR, I WANT SOME MORE! These children are eager to get their four-ounce allowance of sweets.*

1944

DECEMBER
• Civil war erupts in Greece.
• Malmédy massacre in which over eighty US prisoners of war are executed by Waffen-SS troops.
• King George II of Greece declares a regency, leaving his throne vacant.
• Battle of the Bulge begins.

1945

JANUARY
• Auschwitz is liberated by Soviet troops, who find less than 3000 survivors.

FEBRUARY
• Roosevelt and Churchill meet Stalin at the Yalta conference.
• Egyptian premier Ahmed Maher Pasha is killed in parliament after reading a decree.
• USA carries out first firebombing on Tokyo.

MARCH
• Finland declares war on Germany.
• USA carries out second firebombing on Tokyo.
• Würzburg, Germany is 90 per cent destroyed in only twenty minutes by British bombers.
• Soviet Union invades Austria and takes Vienna.

APRIL
• Admiral Suzuki is appointed prime minister of Japan.
• Allies liberate Buchenwald.
• Roosevelt dies and Harry Truman becomes president of the USA.
• Soviet Union enters Berlin.
• Soviet and US troops meet on the Elbe river.
• Mussolini is captured and hanged by Italian partisans.
• USA liberates the Dachau concentration camp.
• Adolf Hitler commits suicide together with Joseph Goebbels.

By 1950 most of the country's food shortages had been dealt with. There were smiles all round when tea was de-rationed in October 1952, and mothers were delighted, as much for themselves as for their children, when sweets stopped being rationed in February 1953. And it was a real red letter day on the calendars of every housewife in Britain when the last foods, butter and meat, were taken off the rations in 1954, and the hated ration books could be thrown away. Food rationing had been in force in Britain for fourteen long years – longer than in any other of the countries caught up in World War II.

Furniture rationing was ended in the summer of 1948, however, it was not until 1953, the year of the new queen's coronation, that the last of the war's furniture restrictions were lifted. In 1946, a continuing lack of materials and workers to make furniture led the government to continue its restrictions on furniture making. At the same time, the range of Utility furniture made was widened, and the restrictions on its sale were relaxed. Now everyone could buy it, provided they had coupons and points. It was finally phased out, but only after a full-scale debate about it in Parliament. The Conservatives, back in government after the 1951 General Election, had wanted to get rid of this vestige of wartime socialism, but Labour MPs had hoped to retain it. Since Utility furniture had been solid and well-designed, and was exempted from Purchase Tax, its departure from the scene was something of a mixed blessing.

Perhaps of greater interest to all women than the lifting of restrictions on food and furniture was the date for when they could throw away their clothes ration books. Even

LATEST PRICES   LATE NIGHT FINAL

ITS CLEAR
Nicholson's
Gin
ITS GOOD

Evening Standard

La Coquille

No. 35,880   LONDON, FRIDAY, SEPTEMBER 1, 1939   ONE PENNY

THE FIRST TELEVISION CHEF

Rationing was still in force when the BBC began giving housewives cookery lessons on television, rather than on the radio. Marguerite Patten, who had worked as a home economist and food adviser during the war, did the cooking on the first BBC Women's magazine programme from November 1947. Although she spent much of her time in front of the television cameras on the early programmes demonstrating how home cooks could make the best of the still restricted ingredients available, quite soon she was able to make use of more exotic foods as they came back into Britain. Brazil nuts came back just in time to be added to Christmas recipes in 1947, for instance. Soon red and green peppers were being seen in shops. Then oranges came back, in small quantities at first but soon in amounts big enough to justify Marguerite's television demonstrations reminding housewives how to make proper marmalade, rather than the preserve made from apples and carrots that had been its wartime substitute.

Television cooks Marguerite Patten and Philip Harben, centre, chat with S.E. Reynolds during one of their programmes.

Queen Elizabeth and her daughters had clothes ration books: when Princess Elizabeth married Prince Philip, Duke of Edinburgh, in November 1947, she had to save coupons to buy the material for her wedding dress.

Women were very tired of their increasingly dreary looking wartime wardrobe, with its pared down fabric content, its few decorative features and its mean use of buttons, pleats and generous lapels. When the French designer Christian Dior sent his New Look clothes down the catwalk in Paris in 1947, British women were astonished and delighted at the length of New Look coats, skirts and dresses, the extravagance of the amount of material used, and the frivolity of its buttons and bows, its hats and its shoes. The Board of Trade was aghast. It could not allow the provision of the materials needed to produce such clothes. British women had to wait another two years for clothes rationing to be ended, in October 1949.

In the plans, agreed months before the war ended, to get servicemen and women home and demobbed, and workers in industry back to their homes in their own part of the country once the war was over, men and women were treated differently. Servicemen, at home and abroad, were given training in various skills, or were able to get qualifications in the teaching profession while still in the forces. Well before demobilisation they were given booklets about 'resettlement advice' and, when they were demobbed, £12-worth of civilian

◀ *EVEN ROYALTY NEEDED COUPONS*
Even Queen Elizabeth II was not exempt from rationing. When she married Prince Philip, Duke of Edinburgh, in November 1947, she had to save coupons to buy the material for her wedding dress.

▲ *NEW LOOK DRESSES*
A teenager tries on a dress with the new post-war longer length skirt, inspired by designer Christian Dior.

clothing, including the infamous 'demob suit', which was 'off coupons' and free of charge.

The planners, feeling that servicewomen might resent have their post-service clothes chosen for them, decided that they should be given cash and coupons to spend as they wished. More then 443,000 women served in Britain's armed forces, at home and abroad, during the war, and it was many months, if not years, before all those who wished to return to civilian life did so. Demobilisation was a quick business for servicewomen – just twenty minutes for WAAF women at RAF Birmingham, Britain's only WAAF demob station – during which the women received their cash and clothing coupons and a leaflet giving them 'guidance' on returning to their post-war, civilian life.

As for women in industry, the first of them to be released from their war-time jobs were housewives needed at home because of

▲ *CIVVIE STREET*
A British soldier pictured after collecting his civilian clothes from the War Office demobilisation shop at London's Olympia. He received a suit, raincoat, shirt, tie, hat, shoes and two pairs of socks with which to enter 'civvie street'

▲ *HOUSEWIVES AND MOTHERS*
Many women chose to leave their jobs and return to being a full-time mother and housewife after the war. Some families had to face living in new prefabricated homes, which were built to cope with the demand after the devastation of war.

family commitments, the wives of demobbed servicemen, and women over sixty. The registration of young, unmarried women in industry was continued, so that there would still be women to replace those who had left. Although many women did stay in their jobs in industry, many chose to return to the lives of housewives and mothers – as they were

HOW WOMEN ACHIEVED THE NEW LOOK

The New Look gave women back their waists and their own shoulder lines and put them in clothes with long sleeves set in tight armholes and ankle-length skirts requiring yards of fabric. There were rows of buttons, and plenty of decoration in the form of sequins, lace, beads and embroidery. Elegantly designed hats were back and shoes had fine, elegant lines and slim, high heels. Still hampered by clothes rationing, women adapted what they had in the wardrobe, or turned, once again, to the precious fabric in old curtains. Skirts were lengthened by adding panels of a contrasting material, often from another, older garment, and, if the skirt was part of a suit, then its jacket, its shoulder pads ripped out, might have had its collars and cuffs covered with the same contrasting material. The waists of dresses were nipped in and old corsets dragged back into use to achieve the tiny, almost Victorian, waist size the style required. Some servicewomen even re-used the corsets that had, to their horror, been given to them as part of their uniform kit when they first joined the services.

A black suede bootee with elastic ankle and pointed collar seen at the first post-war Shoe and Leather Fair held at Olympia, London.

▲ *MEALS ON WHEELS*
A hot meal container is handed over to an elderly woman in her home by a member of the
Women's Royal Voluntary Service as part of the 'Meals on Wheels' service for old people.

being exhorted to do by official propaganda. One year after the end of the war, more than a million women had left their jobs, and by 1951, the numbers of women in employment had dropped back down to pre-1939 levels. Even so, more women were in employment, in proportion to the size of the population, in Britain than elsewhere in Europe.

The contribution of Britain's women to the war effort from 1939 to 1945 and in the immediate post-war years went largely unrecognised for decades. First to get any sort of recognition was the WVS, for which well over a million women had worked during the war. In November 1947, the Home Secretary confirmed that the valuable work the WVS had done throughout the war was still very much needed, and in 1966 it was renamed the Women's Royal Voluntary Service in acknowledgement of the good work it was doing (and still does), especially in hospitals and among the elderly.

MAY 1945
- Germany surrenders.
- Herman Goerring is captured by the USA.
- Heinrich Himmler commits suicide.

JULY
- USA, Britain and France enter Berlin.
- Truman, Stalin and Churchill met at the Potsdam conference to discuss post-war Europe.
- The USA wins the Battle of Okinawa, the last major island battle.

AUGUST
- The nuclear bombing of Hiroshima kills more than 100,000 civilians.
- Soviet Union attacks Japan killing 500,000 Japanese in just two weeks.
- Nuclear bombing of Nagasaki kills more than 100,000 civilians.

SEPTEMBER
- Japan surrenders to China.

OCTOBER
- The winning power create the United Nations.
- Remnants of the Nazi regime are tried at the Nuremberg trials.

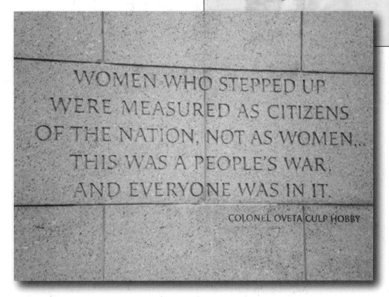

◄ *MEMORIAL TO WOMEN*
The Women of World War II memorial in Whitehall, London.

It was not until the new century that the contribution of women to the war effort was finally officially acknowledged. In July 2005, sixty years after the end of the war, the National Monument to the Women of World War II, erected near the Cenotaph in Whitehall, London was dedicated by Queen Elizabeth II. The uniform the Queen wore as a member of the ATS (which was disbanded in 1948) is among the seventeen sets of clothing and uniforms, symbolising the hundreds of jobs done by women during the war, that are the main feature of the memorial. In 2008, the Women's Land Army's work during the war was acknowledged by the issuing of a special badge, which its recipients could wear at such occasions as Remembrance Sunday. There were still thirty thousand Land Girls alive to receive and wear it, fifty of whom, most of them in their eighties, travelled to London to receive their badge at a reception given by the Prime Minister, Gordon Brown, at No. 10 Downing Street.

▲ *WOMEN'S LAND ARMY VISIT DOWNING STREET*
Prime Minister Gordon Brown talks with former members of the Land Army at Number 10 Downing Street on 23 July 2008 in London. Surviving members of the Women's Land Army and the Women's Timber Corp were presented with Badges of Honour in a ceremony at Number 10. Women volunteered their help in agriculture when male workers went off to fight in World War II. By 1943, 80,000 were working on farms and in forestry.